VERTICAL MIND
PSYCHOLOGICAL APPROACHES FOR OPTIMAL ROCK CLIMBING

©2014 Sharp End Publishing, LLC

Published and distributed by
Sharp End Publishing, LLC
PO Box 1613
Boulder, CO 80306
t. 303.444.2698
www.sharpendbooks.com

ISBN: 978-1-892540-88-1

Library of Congress Catalog: 2013946400

READ THIS BEFORE USING THIS BOOK
WARNING:

Climbing is a very dangerous activity. Take all precautions and evaluate your ability carefully. Use judgment rather than the opinions represented in this book. The publisher and author assume no responsibility for injury or death resulting from the use of this book. This book is based on opinions. Do not rely on information or descriptions, as these are entirely subjective. If you are unwilling to assume complete responsibility for your safety, do not use this book.

THE AUTHOR AND PUBLISHER EXPRESSLY DISCLAIM ALL REPRESENTATIONS AND WARRANTIES REGARDING THIS GUIDE, THE ACCURACY OF THE INFORMATION HEREIN, AND THE RESULTS OF YOUR USE HEREOF, INCLUDING WITHOUT LIMITATION, IMPLIED WARRANTIES OF MERCHANTABILITY AND FITNESS FOR A PARTICULAR PURPOSE. THE USER ASSUMES ALL RISK ASSOCIATED WITH THE USE OF THIS GUIDE.

It is your responsibility to take care of yourself while climbing. Seek a professional instructor or guide if you are unsure of your ability to handle any circumstances that may arise. This book is not intended as an instructional manual.

We dedicate
VERTICAL MIND
to all our wonderful
climbing partners:
past, present,
and future.

Gerry,
I hope you enjoy the book
and find some nuggets to
help you climb with more
confidence!

Contents

Introduction

By Don McGrath

" The fight with your mind is the one you can win only temporarily.
— Adam Ondra, writing about Change, the world's first 5.15c.

You love to rock climb, right? Do you understand why you love it so much? In my first book, *50 Athletes Over 50*, I interviewed older athletes to understand how they stayed at it after so many other athletes had quit participating in sports. I identified that what kept the over-50 athletes engaged in their sports and motivated to train, was joy. In fact, in the book, I isolated four distinct joys by analyzing the data from my interviews with the over-50 athletes. Specifically, the joy of movement, the joy of good health, the joy of accomplishment and the joy of association with other athletes. Further analysis of the data suggested to me that of these joys, the most prevalent for over-50 athletes were the joy of movement and the joy of good health, with the joy of accomplishment and the joy of association being somewhat lower in importance.

Vertical Mind is focused on training for rock climbing and intended to help climbers of all ages. So, when I started work on this book, I decided to see if the same joys were significant motivators for climbers. To do this, I surveyed hundreds of rock climbers, ranging in age from 15 to 60 years, and asked them the following question:

Please rank-order the four joys with respect to how significant they are to keeping you engaged and training for climbing.

More than 180 climbers responded to the survey and the responses are summarized below:

The rank order of the four joys is:

- The joy of accomplishment – 60%
- The joy of movement – 22%
- The joy of good health – 12%
- The joy of association with other climbers – 6%

It appears as though the joy of accomplishment, which psychologists refer to as "competence motivation," is very important to climbers in keeping them engaged in and motivated to train for climbing. Competence motivation is recognized by psychologists as a fundamental and powerful source of human motivation. For me, personally, I love the feeling of reaching my climbing goals. I love even the thought of reaching my climbing goals. I find it very satisfying to send a sport route that I have been projecting. I love sending a traditional route in good style. I love sending a boulder problem that initially seemed impossible for me. I get very inspired by climbing wild features that seem improbable and exciting. The joy of accomplishment provides fuel to sustain this inspiration and translates inspiration into the training and effort required to make those dreams reality.

If you are anything like me or the climbers I surveyed, you want to push yourself. You get inspired by things that either feel or look impossible, or at least appear challenging to you. You get excited by the thoughts and visions of yourself in the throes of doing such things. You anticipate the feeling of joy you will experience when you clip the anchors, grab that finishing jug, or cruise the crux pitch. At some level, you find joy in accomplishing something extreme.

As with nearly all things in life, accomplishments in climbing do not come without training and preparation. And if they do, they're not as satisfying as the accomplishments requiring great effort. I tend to remember most vividly the climbs that required dedication, preparation, and skills to either complete successfully or escape safely. The traditional climbs where my partner and I pushed ourselves out of our comfort zone are often the source of campfire stories. We recount the challenges we faced and how we overcame them. After finishing projects demanding great effort and many attempts, I can often recall fine details of many of the moves for months or years. While explaining why he loved redpointing, Todd Skinner once said, "Flash ascents have flash appeal."

Something that I have grown to appreciate about rock climbing is that success on a climb does not necessarily mean that you made it to the top without falling. Sometimes success is falling, yet learning some lessons along the way. Sometimes success is falling and not completing the climb, but learning or solidifying a critical technique or skill required of the climb. While discussing this topic, co-author Jeff Elison commented that some of the best on-sight climbing he has done was on climbs that he didn't on-sight at all. He climbed some sections really well on-sight, but fell elsewhere. He still viewed these as successes.

Sometimes success is making it back to the ground safely. Obviously, success in climbing has many faces, and the importance or significance of each can be very personal. In this book, I refer to success in climbing as pushing beyond your current self-held limitations or comfort zones. Such successes require both mental and physical training and preparation. The subject of much of this book is how to develop strong connections between your brain and the rest of your body.

Many people have asked me what aspects of their climbing they should focus on for the best and fastest results. These people, mostly weekend warriors like me, have limited time to devote to their training and want to know how to most effectively use it. Many climb one or two days per week, and that constitutes the majority of their rock climbing training. My response to these people, unless I know them well, is "it depends." The focus area that will yield the greatest benefit varies from climber to climber and is dependent on a number of things. This answer is not a very satisfying one, so what I have done in order to be more helpful is define some stages in rock climber development and give some guidelines that can help you understand what may be some areas that could yield the most benefit, given where you are in your development.

Table 1: The Four Stages of Rock Climber Development.

	Novice	Intermediate	Advanced	Elite
Behavior	Learning basic skills	Build repertoire and experiences	Climbing specific training Projecting climbs	Major projecting of hard climbs
Time climbing	< 1 year	<2-3 years	-	-
Climbing/ bouldering level	< 5.8 V0–V2	5.8–5.10 V3–V5	5.11–5.12 V6–V8	5.13–5.15
Fitness level required	Moderate	Moderate	High	Very high
Climbing frequency	1–2 times per week	1–2 times per week	2–4 times per week	3–5 times per week

The columns of Table 1 identify the four stages of rock climber development: novice, intermediate, advanced, and elite. The table also describes various characteristics of climbers in each stage. For example, novice climbers tend to have climbed for less than a year and climb grades up to the 5.7 range. This is not meant to be a hard and fast rule, rather more a guideline, so please do not get too excited if you have been climbing for seven years and climb 5.6. If this is the case, I would tend to think that you have not had climbing as a main focus or pursuit, in which case Table 1 is not accurate. The table also suggests that for this level of climbing only a moderate level of fitness is required and climbers in this stage tend to climb once or twice a week. The table suggests that for this level of climber, the most important training aspects are learning basic footwork techniques and learning to relax and feel comfortable while climbing.

Reviewing Table 1, what stage of climbing development are you in?

I have long been a student of training for rock climbing and have read virtually all the books written in English on the topic. I was a nationally ranked distance runner in college, and from that developed a training mindset. I am familiar with most of the concepts in the literature regarding how to train for rock climbing. I have tried many training plans, some with success and others with no success.

Over the years, I have developed a physical training style that suits my body and works for me and the advanced/elite level at which I currently climb. At age 50, I have found that keeping a high level of general fitness is very important to my climbing. It helps me avoid injuries, recover well from workouts, and to have the general strength and endurance required of the climbing that I like most—hard sport climbing. Given this, I do some sort of resistance or weight training two times per week and some sort of aerobic training two to three times per week. Each of these cross-training workouts lasts about an hour, including the warm up and cool down. I have also found that climbing often (3-4 days per week), and not to exhaustion, yields the best results for me.

While I had more or less refined a physical training program, through trial and error, I had not spent nearly as much time or attention on mental training. As I began consistently climbing at the 5.12+ to 5.13- grades, I began to feel as though it was my mental strength that was holding me back, rather than my physical strength or technique. I found that I would sometimes avoid getting on my project for various reasons, most of which were mental and not physical. For example, I would become preoccupied with a fall, rather than the climbing. I would develop a high level of anxiety when I was close to redpointing a project, and this often would delay my successful completion of the route.

These realizations are why I began studying mental training for rock climbing. My studies revealed many instances from my past where my failures were due to mental factors. I knew I was on the right path to improving my climbing. In the following paragraphs, I describe just a few of the instances that reinforced how my mental state was holding me back more than my physical ability or technique.

I recall an eye-opening event when learning to lead-climb at the 5.12 level. While climbing one day with my good friend and climbing mentor Fred Abbuhl, I was struggling on the crux of a climb named *Eyeless in Gaza* (5.12b). This crux involved making a hard clip from a powerful side pull, followed by small handholds before reaching a good rest position.

I was having a devil of a time making the clip at the crux. I would get into position to clip and immediately get tired and yell "take." After watching me do this four or five times, Fred yelled that I should not be having a hard time with the clip. Like that was helpful!

He told me to forget about the clip and instead climb into the clipping position and see how long I could hold that position. I did this and found that I could stay there for nearly a full minute. Hmmmm. Now, that was helpful! Could it be that my brain was telling me that I was tired, overriding my true physical capability? It certainly seemed so.

Another example occurred the day I finally redpointed my first 5.13. The climb was *Survival of the Fittest*, in the Gunks of upstate New York. I had worked on this climb off and on for over two years before succeeding. I attempted Survival countless times, always learning something that led to my eventual success.

The eye-opening moment came on the day I succeeded. I did the climb without falling, not once, but twice! The same thing happened to me on my second 5.13—*Vasodilator* in Boulder, Colorado. The day I sent this climb, I did so twice.

How is it that a climb that was really hard for me could suddenly seem easy? Clearly, what limited my climbing was my mental fitness.

Think about a hard boulder problem or route that you tried recently, one that seemed impossible, but after a few attempts seemed do-able. Did you really get stronger over the course of a night or a few days? Of course not. The improvements you experienced were due to shifts in your mindset and changes in neuroconnections caused by working that climb.

Over the past few years, I have become convinced that we, as climbers, should spend more of our attention on training our brains. I researched solid and practical mental training for climbing that I could use, and I found relatively little information available.

In order to understand more about which mental factors hold climbers back, I conducted another survey. I asked hundreds of climbers what holds them back most in their rock climbing performance.

A summary of how they responded follows:
- Physical power – 30%
- Fear of falling – 26%
- Technique – 22%
- Physical endurance – 18%
- Fear of failure – 4%

It is interesting that the fear of falling, a mental aspect, is very high on the list. All sports have a mental aspect to them, but one aspect where rock climbing differs from sports such as baseball, bowling, or most running events, is that there is a very real and present fear element. The sports listed, along with many others, do not have nearly as much objective danger as rock climbing. Sure, there is a chance that a pitcher can get drilled by a line drive, but that danger isn't in the forefront of a pitcher's mind in the same way falling or rock fall is in a climber's mind.

Many sports carry with them risks similar to those in rock climbing, including mountain biking, downhill skiing, kayaking, and many others. I mention this, not to call rock climbing out as more dangerous than other sports, but to call attention to the very real need for mental training in climbing and the other sports that carry significant risks. In doing research for this book, I interviewed many rock climbers who climb at the advanced or elite level, and I asked them the question, "How important is your mental state in your rock climbing performance?" Below are some sample responses from this group of climbers.

"For me I think [mental training is] almost everything. If I had to put a number on it, I'd say it's 95%. If you climb consistently and maintain a baseline level of fitness, it seems like your body is always ready. It seems like your body is always up to performing at probably close to your peak physical level. Almost every time I've failed or not pushed through to success, it was because of a mental issue. Either I wasn't trying hard enough, I was scared, I was apprehensive, I didn't put in the proper effort in the first place, or I was distracted." – Matt Samet

"I would say mental strength is of 100% importance to me, because if I'm not totally psyched about a climb, then my performance is not going to be good at all. I might not even get on the climb." – Katie Lambert

I asked this same group of climbers how they mentally train. In spite of their beliefs that mental state is extremely important, few of these climbers spend much time or energy specifically on mental training. I interviewed Arno Ilgner, the author of *The Rock Warrior's Way*, one of the few books on mental training for rock climbers. He said, "Mental strength is crucial for climbing at advanced levels. Very few people can climb beyond 5.10 or 5.11 without falling frequently. Dealing with the fear of falling is one aspect of mental training, and for years climbers have struggled wrapping their brains around how to train for this." He also told me that "You can be physically strong and have great climbing technique, but if you are not also mentally strong, you cannot utilize your strength to climb as hard as you could."

Like Arno, I believe that all climbers can benefit from specific mental training methods. One day, while rock climbing in Rifle, I shared my thoughts and some of what I had found in my research and self-experimentation with Jeff Elison, an accomplished climber and professor of psychology at Adams State University. It turns out that Jeff had been performing research that is well aligned with my thoughts. In addition, he is familiar with a wide variety of branches within psychology, each of which has something to contribute to mental training: cognitive psychology, sport psychology, social psychology, and evolutionary psychology. Very quickly, we decided to put our heads together and produce this book, which represents our collective knowledge. We think this knowledge will help all climbers improve their mental game and their overall climbing performance.

When most of us think of mental training, we envision some-one in a meditative state, practicing visualization, or someone reciting affirmations such as, "I am strong and confident." While these are forms of mental training, they are not the most effective forms. As Jeff and I will discuss in the pages that follow, the most effective mental training develops scripts that enable us to produce flawless movements, focused attention, and productive emotions with high efficiency. Developing such scripts, which involve our brains as well as the rest of our bodies, requires first thinking about what we want to develop, using the safe environment presented by play opportunities, and finally testing ourselves in the cauldron of real life execution.

In the coming chapters, we will provide a review of the science behind how mind-body training works. We'll explain your brain's role in optimal performance and how you need to shift as much of your climbing movement to be automatic responses, requiring little conscious thought. We will explain the psychology behind what makes climbing enjoyable and describe thought patterns and situations that disrupt our ability to have fun, even while doing things that we love.

We will delve into the origins of fear, why it exists and why it is a double-edged sword, both motivating us and holding us back. You will learn about the fear of falling and the fear of failure as the key fears that hold climbers back from higher performance and from experiencing fun in their climbing.

We will present the latest research on how to attain the "zone" or "flow" state. If you've worked at attaining high performance in just about any area of your life, you have probably experienced being in the zone. It's a place of near effortless high performance where you execute flawlessly with total focus in the moment. You will learn about factors that allow you to more reliably reproduce this state while climbing.

We lead you through exercises that will enable you to identify unproductive thoughts or behaviors that are holding you back in your climbing. We offer practical exercises that help you overcome these barriers by replacing them with more productive thoughts and behaviors. We teach you how to bring your newly won skills to bear in improving your climbing performance when you go for that send.

The book is organized to give you an overview of the science behind the topics we explore, with exercises interspersed so that you can work at improving your mental game as you read. We feel that *Vertical Mind* provides unique insights into how to improve your climbing through integrated mind-body training, as well as the theory behind why this training works. For example, in Chapter 2, which forms the basis for the rest of the book, we introduce important brain science that is relevant to learning and high-performance rock climbing. Both Jeff and I learn best when we understand the why behind the how, and we feel that most people learn best this way. We also know that most climbers do not have a lot of time to train. We believe that this book will improve your climbing dramatically without requiring you to spend more time training, because the drills can be integrated into your existing workout schedule.

2 Your Brain and Performance

By Jeff Elison

> **To think is to practice brain chemistry.**
> – *Deepak Chopra*

All training is mental training, quite literally. Any skilled be-havior is learned. Therefore, in this chapter we will describe some of the science behind learning: changes that occur in your brain, formation of habits and skills, and the process of changing bad habits or refining skills. The concepts we cover apply to phys-ical skills, but even more so to mental skills—habits of thought.

Behaviors or movements (e.g., precision flag, overgripping) are the products of neural firing. Neurons in your brain initiate your movements. These neurons tell particular muscles to con-tract or relax via peripheral neurons, which relay the messages from brain-to-muscle. Similarly, all thoughts (e.g., "I'm going to fall") and all emotions (e.g., fear of falling) are the products of firing neurons. Thus, neural firing is responsible for the three domains of psychology: thinking, feeling, and doing. No neural firing and you are without thoughts, feelings, or emotions. You are dead. In fact, it takes many, many neurons firing in particular patterns to produce the end results that we observe as thoughts and feelings. Understanding a bit about how this system works will help your mental training.

First, saying a neuron has *fired* means an electrochemical re-action has occurred. This reaction is the way signals are transmit-ted from neuron-to-neuron or neuron-to-muscle. Second, any specific neuron receives inputs from many other neurons. Some of these are sending signals telling the receiving neuron signals to fire and some are telling it not to fire. At some threshold, a neuron fires in an all-or-nothing fashion. For example, intense fear isn't more intense because the neurons are firing harder. The intensity comes from *more* neurons firing. Third, (and now we are getting somewhere) *Hebb's Law* states that when Neuron A fires, caus-ing Neuron B to fire, changes occur in the neurons that make this firing sequence "easier" or more likely in the future. Some people describe Hebb's Law as: "Neurons that fire together, wire together."

What this means for climbing, and life in general, is that repetition, practice, and drills improve performance by changing neural connections. Since even a simple movement like tapping your finger requires complex patterns of neural firing, practice changes many neurons. Furthermore, we only want to fire the "correct" neurons. Otherwise, when it comes to behavior, we get awkward movements: jerky, imprecise, or overly strenuous. For example, observe the spastic movements of newborns. They attempt to suck their thumbs and end up poking themselves in the eye. As they mature, they master this simple set of movements. This mastery comes from changing patterns of neural firing.

The same thing occurs when we progress as climbers. Our first attempt at a deadpoint may be off the mark, a bit like the infant. We improve by contracting just the right muscles via just the right neurons. Although some people refer to these improvements as "*muscle-memory*," muscles have no memory. All memories are encoded in neurons. Nevertheless, muscle-memory may be a helpful metaphor for what is really occurring—you are teaching your neurons to contract the right muscles in a more coordinated fashion. So, these changes that occur to the neurons are the definition of *learning*!

Thinking works the same way. Studying, practice, and repetition change neurons so that they are more likely to fire together— you learn ideas. The firing becomes faster, more efficient, even automatic and effortless. This is why your third-grade teacher had you spend hours on the times-tables. Now you hear "five times five" and a pattern of neural firing instantly and effortlessly produces the thought "twenty-four"—I mean "twenty-five."

Rehearsing something until it becomes automatic is called *overlearning* or *automaticity*. Think about memorizing beta. Why did that redpoint crux feel so easy after rehearsing it a hundred times? Why was it so much less scary? Rehearsal made you quick and efficient at perceiving the holds, grabbing them exactly the right way, and moving smoothly between them. You weren't searching all over, playing with your grip on every hold, overgripping, or thrutching between holds because you had trained your neurons to fire in efficient patterns. Because you overlearned the sequence, you could reliably produce it under pressure, and you experienced less anxiety. These benefits can be seen in another realm: Overlearning reduces test anxiety and the probability that a student will choke. I discuss fear and choking in more detail in Chapter 4.

An analogy will make the connection between overlearning and neural changes more clear. Recall Hebb's Law: neurons that fire together are more likely to fire together again in the future. By practicing times-tables or beta, we are in a sense beating down a well-worn path. I always tell my students to picture campus right after a foot of fresh snow has fallen. You want to take the short cut from the parking lot to your building. Any route you take is the same—you will be breaking trail. However, the next person is far more likely to follow in your footprints. An hour later, a hundred students have walked that same path and beaten it down to an obvious, easy, clear channel through the foot of snow. Automaticity is the result of neural changes in response to practice. When we practice repeatedly, neural firing is traversing the same route. We are creating paths across neurons, much like a path in the snow. While psychologists prefer the term automaticity, we might call this the *Path Effect*.

The benefits of automaticity go well beyond redpointing, but we will return to those shortly. The issue we need to tackle now is that sometimes we need to learn something new and sometimes we need to unlearn something bad. This applies to patterns of thinking (e.g., self-defeating thoughts) and feeling (e.g., uncontrollable fear) just as much as it applies to smooth technique.

Schemas

You and I cannot see or monitor the firing of individual neurons, nor could we make sense of all the data if we could monitor large numbers of individual firings. So, we need to move up a level or two in terms of organization (Figure 2.1). The next level of interest is what psychologists call *schemas*. A schema is your mental blueprint for an idea. Schemas can be extremely simple or complex. For example, when you recognize the letter "a," your schema for "a" has been activated. When you hear the word "sushi," your schema for "sushi" gets activated. Seeing a chalked undercling should activate your mental skill schemas, allowing you to visualize how to use it. Schemas vary from person to person, so one person may have a complex schema for sushi that includes visions of particular types, a sushi bar, wonderful emotions, and may result in salivation. Another person may turn green.

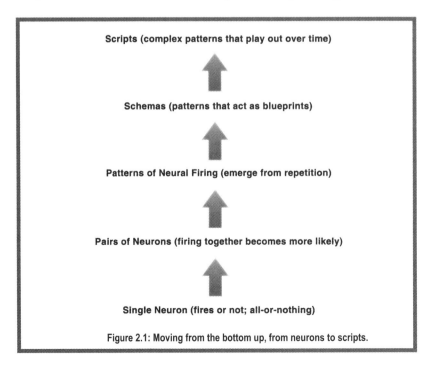

Figure 2.1: Moving from the bottom up, from neurons to scripts.

Schemas help us process information easily, often setting expectations. Imagine the following scenario. You are climbing a wall that overhangs by 20 degrees. You stretch up and grab an in-cut hold at 10 o'clock with your left hand. You feel gravity pull you in a barndoor fashion. I'm guessing that if you are an experienced climber, your backstep (with right foot) schema or flag schema or both were activated before you got to this sentence. So, most of the time, schemas help us think better, faster, and remember more.

As a further illustration of schemas, look at the next page and quickly read the two phrases in Figure 2.2, and then continue reading here. Legend has it that, in elementary school, the famous mathematician Gauss and his classmates were asked by a cranky teacher for the following sum: $1 + 2 + 3 + \ldots + 99 + 100$. She was irritable and wanted to keep them busy and quiet for a long time. After about 30 seconds, as the story goes, Gauss brought her the answer: 5050. He saw the patterns: $1 + 100 = 101; 2 + 99 = 101; \ldots ; 50 + 51 = 101$ and realized the answer was 50×101. Bright boy and an example of pattern recognition, but I really just wanted to distract you and your memory for a few sentences. What phrases did you read on the next page? How about "Shot in the dark" and "Once upon a time"? If that's what you remember, then you are wrong. You've been led astray by your schemas. Check again, carefully. Read each and every word aloud and slowly, if you need to.

Schemas can have a down side. We may perceive what we expect, rather than reality. They can also make us miss things. These problems apply to climbing and everyday life. Because they embody (literally in terms of neural coding) our expectations, we may make mistakes or get locked into a single approach to a problem (e.g., crux moves, fear).

Figure 2.2: Reading and Schemas.

Scripts

Schemas are interesting and apply to climbing, but if we want to understand habits (good and bad), we really need to move up one more level of complexity to *scripts*. By "habits" I mean repeated behaviors (e.g., overgripping, spotting sly kneebars), repeated thoughts (e.g., "I'm not good enough to get on this climb"), and repeated emotions (e.g., "The presence of all those good climbers makes me feel inferior"). Scripts are a bit like schemas played out over time. In fact, the distinction can be subtle. In *Performance Rock Climbing*, Dale Goddard and Udo Neumann refer to "motor engrams," possibly due to their emphasis on technique and strength training. Because of our focus on mental training, we use the term scripts, which encompasses repeated patterns of thinking and feeling, in addition to movements. Just as schemas have their pros and cons, so do scripts. However, scripts embody more complex situations and offer the key to improvement: we can learn new scripts and unlearn harmful ones.

Brains, especially human brains, have evolved to perceive patterns—whatever makes this situation similar to previous situations. Who or what were the key players? How did I, or other people, or animals, or things behave? Generally, this is a very positive mechanism. It allows us to respond automatically, quickly, and efficiently. These sequences of perceptions / thoughts / feelings / actions are what cognitive psychologists call scripts. The term comes from playwriting since scripts specify the characters, actions, emotions, motivations, and expectations of the "drama." They may be as mundane as your morning routine or what you do when you bump into someone trying to walk through a doorway. Or they may be as important as your way of interacting with loved ones or responding in emergency situations. For example, the novice driver does not instinctively turn into the direction of a skid, but the experienced driver does this before she even registers consciously what is going on. The experienced climber backsteps automatically, quickly, efficiently, without deliberate conscious analysis. The experienced typist presses the appropriate keys without looking at the keyboard or wasting conscious thought on where the keys are. These examples point to the adaptive aspects of scripts.

Scripts explain more than just habits of thinking, feeling, and behaving. They include patterns in general. For example, you might not refer to your trip to work or school as a habit, but it is definitely scripted. You have expectations about what you are going to see (e.g., stop lights), what you are going to do (e.g., turn at Elm St.), and you can make the trip with little conscious effort. Scripts also include things we have learned but not yet experienced. For example, you may have knowledge and expectations of what it would be like to be a cop or a professional climber or married. That knowledge and those expectations are scripted and may drive our thinking, feeling, and behavior when we later end up in those situations. There's a joke that captures this well: Marriages are doomed when men learn about sex from pornography and women learn about love from romantic comedies. Neither source represents reality, so both lead to disappointment when these unrealistic expectations become scripted.

Why We Need Scripts

Scripts are typically automatic, quick, and efficient. As such, we usually carry them out reliably, in the same or similar way every time. Moreover, they require little conscious effort, allowing us to conserve valuable resources: attention, consciousness, and *working memory*. Attention, consciousness, and working memory are very intimately linked and very limited. On average, a human adult can hold about 5-9 items in working memory (a newer, more accurate term for short-term memory). Working memory is the bottleneck in thinking. As such, individual differences in working memory predict intelligence, as do differences in attention. These individual differences are partially hereditary (i.e., good genes) and partially learned (i.e., concentration). One of our greatest adaptations is the ability to learn, to practice, and to turn conscious working-memory intensive tasks into automatic scripted tasks. This is the automaticity I mentioned previously.

Perhaps you can still remember how mentally exhausting it was to drive a car. Now you drive miles and miles, navigating turns, stop signs, stop lights and more, barely conscious of what you are doing. Instead, you have attention and working memory to spare for talking to a passenger or learning lyrics from your new CD. Similarly, the skilled typist can think about more important things than typing. He can think about flow of ideas, topic sentences, summary sentences, and segues. Practice and familiarity improve performance, create automaticity, and reduce the load on working memory and attention. That is why so many moves on your project feel easy and automatic after 20 attempts. By sparing working memory and attention, we can improve performance—often in spite of our genes. Unfortunately, at other times, practice makes our *mistakes* habitual!

Simply put, practice turns the explicit (conscious, deliberate) into the implicit (unconscious, automatic). Patterns of neural firing become highly probable, easily initiated, and reliably executed. As an illustration, if you are a good typist, finding the keys is an implicit skill. But it wasn't always so. At first you had to hunt for them. If you are a good climber on overhanging terrain, you grab that sidepull and implicitly look for a foothold on which to backstep. But as a novice, you had to figure it out or get beta from others.

For the goals of this book, two points about scripts are important. First, scripts involve habits of thought, behavior, and emotion. Yes, fear—of falling or failure—may be habitual and may drive our maladaptive behaviors (e.g., overgripping). Just as schemas can lead us to make errors—"see" and remember the wrong thing, such as "Shot in the dark"—scripts can work against us in even more complex and important ways. Second, if you want to make changes, you are talking about changing scripts.

So You Want to Make a Change?

We all have things we aren't happy about: failures, falls, bad habits, procrastination... Most of us can easily identify things about ourselves that we would like to change. We also have habits or flaws in our climbing technique of which we may be unaware. This makes sense since habits are scripts and scripts may be implicit, unconscious, and automatic. Sometimes a coach or helpful significant other will point them out: "Why the hell do you chew like a cow?" These observations about scripts lead to a general process for making changes.

Steps for Changing Scripts

First, you have to become aware of problematic scripts and choose new scripts to replace the bad ones:

1. Raise to consciousness: I need to know I'm doing it; a coach, video, or friends can help.
2. Pick an alternative—"what should I do instead?" (Then, step back from performance situations, practice and play with new techniques or scripts).
3. Catch yourself when you are about to follow the old script and replace it with the new one.
4. Repeat Step #3 over and over and over. Practice drills in a safe, even fake environment. You may even want to exaggerate your response!
5. In the final step, you put your new scripts into practice where it matters. Practice in the affective environment! Affective means emotional, under stress, in the heat of the moment.

Now, let's delve deeper into this process and examine some of the science behind changing scripts.

Building on existing theory, psychologist Albert Ellis developed a process to help people identify and change maladaptive patterns. His original ABC model has been extended to D and E, but let's start simply with the first step: C. C represents Consequences, the things we don't like. These negative consequences may be our anger, feeling bad about ourselves, or failing to achieve our goals. That's right, C is first in the *process* of making changes. A and B come before C chronologically, but we aren't interested in every ABC, just the C's that bother us. So, we start there, where we become conscious of something we want to change.

Identifying Consequences sounds simple and sometimes it is, but applied to climbing, we sometimes have to dig deeper. For example, let's say you don't like falling. That makes sense, but now dig a little and ask yourself why do you fall? Because you aren't strong enough? That's an easy answer. There are many reasons climbers fall that end in "I wasn't strong enough." Picking just one, as a working example, it is often because we overgrip. If I can identify something like overgripping as a Consequence, then I've done this more than once, probably often. In fact, I probably do it unconsciously and automatically. Therefore, my brain has created a script, and it is that script that I need to change.

Ellis would now have us jump to A: the Antecedents, the things that "cause" the Consequence. When do you overgrip? Under what conditions? Maybe it is when you are 3' or 5' or 10' above a bolt. Maybe it is when you have put pressure on yourself to onsight or send THIS go. Let's go with the latter. Now we have a summary statement: "When I feel pressure to send NOW, I overgrip."

Figure 2.3 illustrates the general ABC process. Figure 2.4 captures our climbing-specific example of falling due to overgripping.

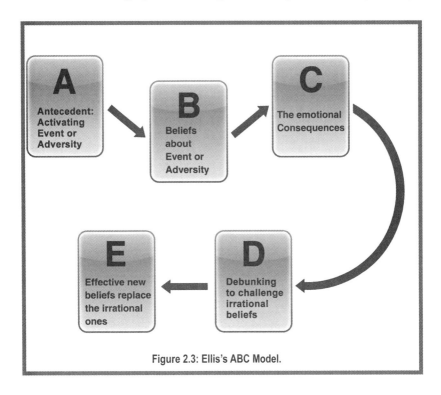

Figure 2.3: Ellis's ABC Model.

Ellis explains that we do things, even bad habits, for a reason—or multiple reasons. Often we are not explicitly conscious of these reasons. We may have developed implicit beliefs without knowing it. To understand explicit versus implicit here, compare these two things you know: Who was the first president of the United States versus what are the rules of grammar? We explicitly know the president, meaning we can "explicate it." We are conscious of the answer and we can put it into words: Samuel Adams? Or did he invent beer? In contrast, we know the rules of grammar implicitly: we use them constantly but we are not conscious of most of them and cannot put them into words.

B stands for "beliefs." These are the reasons, explicit or implicit for why we do what we do. Not surprisingly, B comes between A and C. In other words, some situation (i.e., Antecedent = pressure) triggers Beliefs that lead to an undesired result (i.e., Consequence = falling). Any ABC sequence that you tend to repeat is a script. Uncovering the ABC's is an effective technique for achieving Step 1: raising our scripts to consciousness.

Returning to Beliefs, Ellis argues that these intervening beliefs often are not rational, especially the implicit ones. Continuing with our pressure-leads-to-overgripping example, what might some of our beliefs be? One, if I don't crush this hold, I'll fall. Two, other people will think less of me if I fall. And we could probably list many others. To understand Ellis's method, let's just focus on the first one: falling.

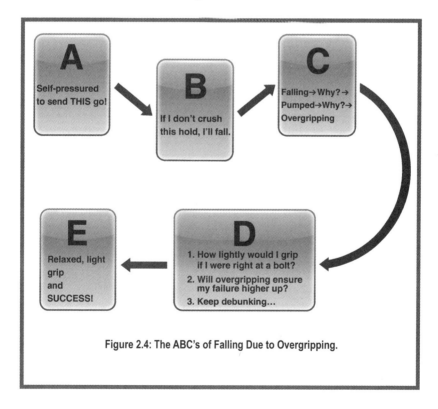

Figure 2.4: The ABC's of Falling Due to Overgripping.

The next step is "D" (Debunking), to question the rationality of these beliefs. What is the evidence in favor of them? What is the evidence that counters them? Usually we can come up with at least a short list, if not a long one. Is it necessary to crush this hold to prevent falling? Probably not! Exhibit One: How many times have you been at a clipping stance, pumped, getting more pumped, crushing that hold to make the clip—and as soon as you do and feel safe, you find that you can rest on those same holds? Maybe crushing it wasn't necessary. Maybe you could have taken two seconds to relax, loosen your grip, reduce your pump, and then clip. That's what Ellis calls counterevidence. The more the better. Exhibit Two: Think about a route you have wired, one you've climbed dozens of times. How hard do you grip those holds? Probably half as hard, or more likely one-tenth as hard as you did on the onsight. If you don't need to crush them now, then you obviously didn't need to crush them then. As they say on the infomercials: "but wait, there's more." You may explicitly or implicitly be thinking you need to crush that hold in case your foot slips. Fair enough, that may be a valid reason. Then again, is that "reason" driven by "emotion": fear of falling, pain, or fear of failure? We can start a whole new line of questioning those beliefs—and we will, later.

For now, let me wrap up with the idea of tradeoffs or cost-benefit analysis. Yes, crushing that hold may safeguard you in the event of a foot slip, but at the same time, it may guarantee your failure/fall a few moves or bolts higher. In the end, you may have to make the decision that your chances of success are optimized by climbing with a light grip, keeping your fear (of pain or failure) in check, and risking a fall due to a slip in exchange for the send. Ultimately, success or improvement is "E"—the new (positive) Emotional experience.

Of course, making changes is easier said than done. None of us can go from a chronically overgripping headcase to climbing like Chris Sharma simply by sitting in a chair analyzing our ABC's. There is more to it, mostly practice, to which we now turn.

Practice & Drills—to Build New Skills (Steps 3 and 4)

Ellis's process, in my simplistic presentation above, sounds a bit like a once-and-done deal. It most certainly is not. Changing habits is not easy. Recall that the pattern of neural firings for the old script has been executed many, many times. Hebb's law says they will probably fire again, unless you work hard to beat down a new path that is easy to follow automatically. That's where Steps 3 and 4 come in.

In Step 1, you or a coach or a partner made you consciously aware of what you have been doing (repeatedly). In Step 2, you have to pick an alternative—what you should be doing. We will suggest specific alternatives for specific problems later in the book. You might also turn to better partners, watch top climbers (live or in videos), or turn to a coach. Now that you are aware of your problematic script and have picked an alternative, you have to repeatedly catch yourself when you are about to execute the old script (habit). Think of these as opportunities to practice by substituting the new script (Step 3). "My instinct and fear tell me to crush this hold, but thanks to Dr. Ellis, I realize I'd be better served by relaxing." This is great, but psychological research offers us even more specific suggestions.

In Step 4, we need to practice over and over. We need to put Hebb's Law to work for us. We need to beat down a path that will be easier to follow, possibly even followed automatically. A famous gymnastics coach said his gymnasts had to execute a routine without error one hundred times in practice before he would allow them to try it in competition. There are three specific ways to get results quickly in Step 4. These are to create opportunities to practice new scripts, learn new scripts under ideal conditions, and exaggerate the new script to obliterate the old one. In the next sections, we explore each of these in turn, offering specific suggestions.

Create Opportunities to Practice New Scripts

Random climbing isn't likely to present us with opportunities to systematically change specific scripts. So, we need to create opportunities to practice new scripts. When and where?

Here are four concrete suggestions.

1. For starters, who cares if you "send" the pink route at the gym? Practice your new scripts/techniques on plastic. Sticking with the example of overgripping, climb easy and hard routes with the lightest touch. Play with that fine line between making it and falling. Big deal if you slip. You may be surprised at what you can get away with and how much strength you save.

2. What about your warm ups? Don't just go through the motions. Make the most of that time. Again, play with the light grip, try being as relaxed as possible, try moving faster. Try "optional" techniques such as heel-hooking or flagging where you don't normally need to. Can you find places where they work?

3. Early season or after a break or injury. You are not close to peaking and you shouldn't be redpointing or trying hard onsights. So, make use of this time to practice what you might not normally do—those new scripts.

4. Make up drills, pick specific routes, or set routes/boulder problems designed for practicing new techniques.

Many years ago, I was living in Fort Collins with a full-time job and a newborn daughter. My climbing time was limited. I spent way too much time bouldering on the crimpers of Rotary Park at Horsetooth Reservoir. As a Consequence (the C in ABC's), I had tendonitis off-and-on for two years. A friend, Herm Feissner, recommended that I work on my open-grip and open-crimps. Yes, it would be a setback for my performance, but it was December and I had months of mostly indoor climbing before I'd be trying harder routes outdoors. He suggested I commit to holding anything I could even imagine holding as an open-grip. If I failed, big deal. I followed that advice for several months and could not believe the gains. Now, as an old(ish) man, I'm incredibly thankful for that advice. I rarely crimp. At that time, I wouldn't have believed the holds I can open-grip, even now being older and less powerful. Moreover, I'm absolutely sure that making the change reduced my injuries.

Learn New Scripts Under Ideal Conditions

Initial learning, what cognitive psychologists call the acquisition phase, should occur under ideal conditions. That begs the question, what is ideal? Easy is ideal—at first. The stress of difficult climbing makes learning and practicing new techniques even more difficult. We will get there, but that's what Step 5 is all about. Let's look at an analogous situation. Imagine you want to give up alcohol. Is it wise to implement this plan for the first time at your best friend's raging New Year's Eve party? Probably not. Similarly, is the best time to try your first dropknee at the end of a 30-foot runout with potential to peg that ledge below you? I'm thinking, probably not—for multiple reasons. Emotion, behavior, and thinking are intimately intertwined, so it is difficult to present all these mental training ideas in a sequential fashion.

Later, we will present the positive and negative effects of fear. But for now, it is sufficient to understand that fear has several negative effects on performance and learning. So, let's minimize fear in this initial acquisition phase.

How does minimizing fear and stress translate to concrete suggestions?

1. For starters, top-roping can be your friend. If you want to improve, don't let your macho badassness get in the way of optimal training. Top-roping reduces risk and fear. It allows you to safely play and experiment with new techniques. It allows you to practice that dropknee, move through it, jump off, and practice it again, immediately! Don't spoil onsighting some coveted route, but if you are in the gym or repeating some warm up, then who cares? Top-rope it and work on your technique or mind control.

2. Another reason we fear falling is because we associate it with failure and negative judgments from other climbers (e.g., embarrassment). So, "safe" may mean emotionally safe. Who is around, who are you climbing with when you stick your neck out there and try to practice new scripts? Does it matter? Of course it does; we are human. Pick a setting that makes it safe to fall or look silly. Pick a partner who will understand. Explain what you are doing. Get them to play along. They will probably benefit as well.

3. "Safe" and "easy" may go together, but they are not the same thing. For example, we can climb very difficult moves on top-rope, making them safe and difficult at the same time. So, our last suggestion here is to practice on easier routes/easier moves. Try that dropknee on an easy

route, when you aren't pumped, when the holds scream how obvious it is. Look for two big holds about 20-some inches apart and try a kneebar. Watch someone else successfully do moves you are learning and replicate them in the same spot. You need to understand how a technique (e.g., kneebar) works and feels, then replicate it, then eventually you will find them on your own.

Many years ago, I realized I could improve by learning from better climbers. Not just hanging out with them or trying to keep up with them, but by explicitly analyzing what they were doing. I remember watching Ken Duncan on a 5.12 at Shelf Road when I hadn't done many 5.12s. On this particular route, I was able to scramble up to a ledge 40 feet above the ground, level with the crux. From there I was able to watch and analyze Ken's technique from a close vantage point. He grabbed the same holds and used a similar sequence as I had. My conclusion: "Wow, I guess you don't get pumped if you just relax your way up the climb." The ease with which he floated the route was due entirely to mental factors.

A month later, I watched Ken climb a 5.11+ at our local gym with flawless technique. In response to my comment about it, he said "Good technique is easy when you aren't pumped." And that's the point of suggestion 3: It's hard to do the right thing under duress, so practice it when you are comfortable, when the meter isn't racing. For many years, psychologists have known that stress or high levels of arousal/anxiety increase the probability of the "dominant response." How does that translate to climbing and our script-theory framework? It means we are more likely to practice the new (non-dominant) script under non-stressful conditions. Conversely, at the end of that runout, we are likely to revert to our old, automatic (dominant) response. So, practice when you are comfortable. Don't let your ego make you afraid to regress a little bit in order to improve in the future, like my months of open-grip climbing. It will just hold you back. That's a nice segue to our third general tactic—Exaggerate!

Exaggerate the New Script to Obliterate the Old One

Our example of climbing with the lightest possible grip, even to the point of falling, overlaps with this tactic. If we want to change something we have been doing habitually, automatically, then we are often most successful by overcompensating or exaggerating a different response. Athletes in other sports go through this all the time.

We can learn a lot from athletes and coaches in other sports and from our own experience with other sports. Most principles of training and optimal performance transcend the specifics of our sport. I'm going to present an example that takes us all the way back to Step 1. I started climbing way before sport climbing existed. In the late '80s, two things lowered my motivation. First, I had achieved a number of my big goals: Half Dome, El Capitan, onsighting *The Naked Edge*. Second, I had a demanding job. At that time, I discovered triathlons. While I had plateaued to some extent in climbing, I found I could improve in three sports at the same time with the net result of increasing my overall triathlon performance. It was addicting, period! My best event was swimming, so that's where I hit my first plateau. At the suggestion of a friend, I hired a coach to watch me swim, videotape me, and offer suggestions. That tape and his analysis were Step 1: raise to consciousness. He made me aware of some obvious flaws in my technique (stroke) that were invisible to me when my face was in the water and I was only imagining what my body was doing relative to the water. Step 2 was easy: He told me what to do and showed me video of much better swimmers.

Step 3 was easy: I knew I was screwing up on every single stroke. Recall that automaticity/overlearned behaviors are automatic and *reliably repeated*—good or bad! Just one of my mistakes was to "windmill" my arm through the air when I was moving it forward. This had a number of bad consequences: wasting energy, over-rotating my body, and driving me deeper into the water. So, I just needed to stop it, right? He didn't just ask me to stop it; he had me crush that old habit. He had me do lap after lap after lap of drills. I had to drag my fingertips through the water with every single stroke. That forced me to keep my hands down and my elbows up. My fingers dragging on the water provided proprioceptive feedback that I wasn't screwing up. In other words, I could tell by feel, without watching myself, that my arm was in approximately the correct position. In summary, he had me *exaggerate* a new response (script) in order to replace that old one.

What was the effect? Total groin-kick to my ego (because that's where he resides). I could barely swim a lap. I went from being able to swim two miles non-stop to struggling to finish a lap. My times at any distance were dismal. What we had done was to turn the implicit into the explicit. It was conscious, new, not automatic, and those neural pathways were not optimal. I was like the infant poking itself in the eye when it wanted to suck its thumb. But, "praise Science," as they say on *South Park*; with practice those drills paid off. New neural pathways, new movement scripts were etched into my brain and peripheral neurons (i.e., what some people call muscle-memory), overriding the old scripts. After a few weeks of continual practice, the explicit transferred to the implicit. The movements became automatic and efficient. Suddenly, I was swimming as fast as I had with my flawed stroke. And from that point, my times dropped *consistently*. I swam four personal bests in a two-week period. I trimmed three minutes (over 10%) off my mile time. Imagine improving your redpoint or onsight performance 10% in a month, just by changing technique. It *is* possible!

My experience with that painful path to improvement is not unique. In fact, it is common for athletes who understand this process and are willing to face short-term periods of lesser performance for long-term improvement. You may recall that Tiger Woods made the conscious, deliberate decision to change his swing back in 2003. He went through a slump, but returned with a vengeance, regaining the rank of first in Official World Golf Rankings. This wasn't the first time he bit the bullet for long-term gains. He changed his swing back in 1997 and experienced a slump in 1998. Starting in 1999, he dominated the sport for one of the longest periods in golf history.

Again, if you want long-term results, don't let your ego stand in the way. Suck it up and accept some short-term setbacks if they will lead to long-term gains. We are breaking implicit habits with this process. We make them explicit and replace them with new habits. Those new habits are not automatic and smooth. They require conscious effort. But with practice, we drive them back to the level of automaticity where we perform them reliably, smoothly, without conscious effort. This in turn frees up consciousness for more important decision making.

Step 5: Under the Gun

In Step 5, we must practice in the "affective environment." The what? Affective means emotional, maybe stressful, maybe scary. So you visualize over and over again how you are going to approach the boss and demand a raise. You have rehearsed what you will say and imagined her possible objections. And then you have to follow through—actually confront her face-to-face, with all the emotions, yours and hers. Or you have visualized skipping that dogger's bolt on the redpoint. You've never taken that whipper, but you think you are ready. You have mentally practiced staying calm and ignoring the fall. Or you have analyzed your overgripping, practiced your light touch and relaxation in the gym and on warm ups, and now you have to stick to your new script on this onsight attempt. You are "under the gun"; this is where the "rubber meets the road"; this is where you are done "talking the talk" and you need to "walk the walk."

At some point, you may just have to go through with it—see if you can pull it off. However, we can often build up to the final test in steps. For example, say your hardest onsight is 5.12c. You can practice your new mental skills incrementally. If you honed them pre-season, then put them to the test on your first 11c of the year, and then some 11d's, and then . . . work your way up. If you've been mentally training to prepare for skipping that dogger's bolt and the potential 40-foot whipper, then you can climb up to the bolt and jump off without going farther. Then climb a few feet above and jump off under control. We will return to this later, but the point is that you can practice and solidify your gains under increasingly stressful situations. This has advantages. Fear is easily learned and reinforced. If you think you have conquered it on the couch or in the gym and you rush out and get burned by going for broke, you may end up erasing all those gains. "I've watched NASCAR, so I'm sure I can take my minivan around this mountain hairpin at 70 mph..."

Be introspective, be self-aware. If you are nervous about other things, if you are distracted, if you are feeling tired, then don't go for broke. Don't rush it. Don't risk a setback. Putting new scripts to work for you, when you are under the gun, requires that you be on top of your game. A growing body of psychological research demonstrates that self-regulation of behavior (e.g., dieting) and emotion (e.g., fear) is a limited resource, just like muscular strength. For example, dieters who are stressed at work, who have to self-regulate their emotions or attention at work, are more likely to break down and cheat on their diets. Similarly, if you are stressed about work or factors outside your climbing, it may be harder to stick to your new scripts, to keep fear in check, to relax when that is what you need to do.

Instinctual Drift and Spontaneous Recovery

I'm all about setting realistic expectations. They help us cope with and accept less than ideal performances, setbacks, or times when we regress. For example, how many of us finish a season or come off our peak feeling confident, with little fear of a typical sport-climbing fall. Then we rest for a month, or perhaps injury or bad weather forces us to take even more time off. We come back to climbing and that confidence isn't the same. Our fear is greater. Have we regressed? Sort of. Understanding two important principles of psychology may help you anticipate these changes, accept them, and save you from beating yourself up over these minor setbacks.

Psychologists, being the fun bunch of nerds that we are, taught pigs to pick up wooden coins, carry them across their pen and deposit them in piggy banks. Get it? Pigs and piggy banks . . . how cute. The researchers used some of the same principles we will be talking about, in particular, reinforcement. The pigs were rewarded for doing this. Psychologists prefer the word "reinforced" for several reasons. When we are reinforced, the probability of the reinforced behavior increases. Learning occurs. However, some things come naturally, instinctively. They are easier to learn or some don't even need to be learned. Others are harder to learn because they are counter to instincts or unnatural. Pigs naturally root, meaning they tend to push things around in the dirt with their snouts. Pigs don't make deposits in piggy banks naturally or instinctively. When the researchers stopped re-inforcing this behavior, the pigs went back to doing what pigs do—rooting. They stopped making deposits and went back to burying the coins in the dirt. *Instinctual drift* is the term psychologists use for the pigs' return to behaviors that came naturally.

Fear of heights and falling is instinctive for humans. Evolution has predisposed us to learn fear of heights and spiders and snakes more easily than fear of electricity and guns. Although the latter two kill far more humans, they are too new for evolution to have shaped our instincts toward them. So, fear of heights is instinctual and learning to love heights is less natural. Learning to enjoy and relax while climbing at great heights requires more work. So, humans, just like the pigs, tend to experience instinctual drift. If we have not been climbing for a while, we may start rooting like pigs—not really. If we have not been reinforced for staying calm and keeping our fear in check, then we may drift back to being fearful. The bottom line is that each new season or each hiatus may force us to face our fears once again and require more practice. It is likely that we will have to return to Steps 3-5.

Spontaneous recovery is similar in that old responses or scripts may regain a foothold on our minds. Imagine you un-learn a response. Pavlov's dogs learned to salivate when they heard a bell because it meant food was coming. However, some of the dogs unlearned this response (called extinction) by hearing the bell over-and-over without getting food. This is analogous to us un-learning an old script and replacing it with a new one (e.g., stop overgripping). Then after months of not hearing the bell at all, they suddenly heard it again. How did they respond? The "extin-guished" salivation response came back—spontaneous recovery. This is analogous to us taking months off from climbing. In the absence of exposure to heights and the absence of us implementing our new scripts, the old scripts (e.g., fear, overgripping) may return spontaneously. We feel like we have had a setback.

I bring this up for two reasons. First, set your expectations. This is normal. Don't beat yourself up over apparent regression. Second, another psychological finding may make this pill less bitter to swallow. The setback doesn't take you all the way back. Thousands of studies show that *relearning* is faster than initial acquisition. As examples, you probably learned a foreign language or algebra in high school. Many of us have not used these skills and feel like we "forgot everything." That is incredibly unlikely. Studies show that some learning from even extremely brief (even subliminal) experiences persists at an unconscious level for 20 years or more. Most people who have learned a foreign language can relearn it in less than half the time that it took to learn originally. So, you can relearn those new climbing scripts and make them your dominant response, with far less work and time.

I'm old enough that I remember the days before climbing walls. I can vividly remember returning to Smith Rock in the mid-1980s after a winter away from climbing. My first route of the year was three whole number grades below my best onsight, but it still scared the hell out of me. I came down to the ground wondering why I liked climbing. Or if I even liked it at all? By the end of that same day, I had onsighted a route just one number grade below my max, and I was in love again. What had I been thinking? Climbing is the best. Spontaneous recovery of fearful scripts and instinctual drift toward fear were replaced by rapid relearning. Those scripts of mind control that we all thrive on came back after a half a dozen routes.

Returning to the Path Effect, instinctual drift and spontaneous recovery are like snow blowing across the new path while we weren't taking that route. The new snow may cause us to reroute our course to older paths. Fortunately, the snow only partially covers the new path. Relearning is faster because the path is still there. We just need to walk that route a few times to beat it down and get back to where we left off.

Climb Harder, Have More Fun

In the chapters that follow, we examine common problems that keep climbers from reaching their potential and reduce their enjoyment. Issues like fear of falling and fear of failure impact both performance and fun. These fears and our reactions to them are scripted. Now that you understand something about brains, neurons, and scripts, we will apply the principles of scripts, automaticity, and Ellis's ABC process to improving your mental game. This means identifying problem scripts, reducing their power, and replacing them with more productive scripts.

Physical training will enhance performance and may even make your climbing more fun, but mental training directly targets both goals. Furthermore, mental training can be practiced in parallel with physical training for the greatest gains. Your body may limit the number of hours you can boulder, or you may have reached a plateau in your physical training. However, mental training provides a whole new route to success, one you can practice seven days a week without fatigue, one that is sure to produce gains and move you beyond a current plateau.

3 Your Brain and Fun

By Jeff Elison

> **"The best surfer out there is the one having the most fun.**
> – *Duke Kahanamoku*

> **"The best climber in the world is the one having the most fun.**
> – *Alex Lowe*

Most of us have had the experience of trying to explain why we climb, or worse yet, justifying ourselves to skeptical friends or family. They don't just want to know why we do it; they want to know how we can justify "wasting" all our free time and money on climbing. Or how we justify putting ourselves in danger. Or why we choose to inflict the pain and discomfort on ourselves. I had an ex-girlfriend (emphasis on ex-) who couldn't understand why I would even want to "try so hard" at anything physical. The pain, time, and money were way beyond her comprehension. So, why do we climb? What motivates us? What are the payoffs?

This chapter will explore some psychological explanations that apply to why people find themselves motivated to do many challenging things, including dangerous sports. Of course our emphasis will be on climbing—how this knowledge can be used to increase performance and enjoyment.

Let's face it, when we make statements like climbing is "fun" or that it makes us "happy," we may be misleading other people. We are taking a broader perspective when we say these things. For example, were you happy and having fun when your forearms were screaming in pain and your mind was filled with fear over the 20' whipper you were facing? Probably not. But after you pulled off that crux move, climbed to the anchor, lowered to the ground, de-pumped, de-stressed . . . and looked back at your experience, THEN you were happy and having fun. When you got back to camp, downed a beer, and told (or likely re-told) the story, THEN you were really having fun!

Subjective Well-Being

The point is this: Happy and fun are rather simplistic words that we apply to complex real-life experiences. Psychologists have recognized this point and have a more encompassing term:

subjective well-being. Most of us say we want to be happy, but the psychologists who study these things (members of the Positive Psychology movement) have largely given up studying happiness and turned to subjective well-being. They realize that there is more to "the good life" than moments of joy. There are other important emotions involved. They know that being interested and excited about what you are doing, right now, makes life better. They know that pride in overcoming challenge and adversity (e.g., pumped arms and fear) makes life better. They know that being completely immersed in the moment makes life better. So, the reasons why climbing is so damn fun are many, varied, and sometimes complex.

When we discuss "flow" in Chapter 10, we will see that the originator of the flow theory, Csíkszentmihályi, believes "a good life is one that is characterized by complete absorption in what one does."

Motivation Theories

Many theories and models have been advanced to explain individual differences in motivation. They are intended to explain why certain people do and enjoy certain things. Several theories are especially applicable to rock climbing. Some theories help us understand why certain people choose to endure hard training, painful climbs, repeated failures, living in a tent, and poverty in order to climb more or harder. Some theories help us understand why certain people climb even when they don't care about performance or why some people climb when they know they won't ever again climb as hard as they once did. Multiple theories may describe each of us, because most of us are driven by multiple motives. In addition, these theories are not mutually exclusive—they overlap in some areas.

Optimal Arousal Theory is based on the observation that we like neither boredom nor overstimulation. We have some ideal range in which we prefer to operate. If under-aroused, we feel bored and seek out something to make life more interesting or even exciting. If over-aroused, we feel anxious or stressed and try to escape or alter the situation. Novelty and unfamiliarity contribute to arousal. The optimal range of arousal or stimulation varies from person to person. Some of us are set on low, others set on high. Perhaps counter-intuitively, a setting for high arousal may be because we are biologically less reactive. For example, we are excited or frightened less easily and become bored more easily than other people. Therefore, we need more frequent, more intense, or more unusual experiences to overcome boredom.

Applied to climbing, we may seek to overcome the boredom of work and everyday life by increasing our arousal levels with a little excitement or even fear. Conversely, we may seek to escape the stress of work and bad relationships in a relaxing environment. Because novelty increases arousal, some of us are bored by climbing the same routes, in the same areas, over and over. We try to maintain optimal arousal by traveling and onsighting.

Evolutionary Theory might be seen as a modern refinement of *Instinct Theory*. Both suggest that some motives and behaviors are genetic, inherited. They do not need to be learned. They are evolutionary adaptations. We like sex because our ancestors who liked sex had more kids than our ancestors who did not like sex. Preferences are in part hereditary, so the preference for sex became more common in our gene pool, a part of human nature. The same story explains our preferences for fat and sugar. Ancestors who liked fatty and sweet foods were less likely to starve and as a result were more likely to reproduce, increasing the preference for fat and sugar.

Applied to climbing, we may enjoy climbing and swinging from our arms because ancestors who mastered climbing were more likely to survive. Look at kids on the playground. They seem to love the monkey bars for no reason. Climbers are just big kids who haven't lost touch with our evolutionary roots. Play itself is seen as an evolutionary adaptation. Children improve their coordination, physical fitness, health, and social awareness via play. Play as an adaptation isn't limited to humans. Behaviors that can only be described as play have been observed in a variety of other species. The benefits are similar to those enjoyed by humans. We lucky climber-adults are still able to let ourselves play, enjoy it, and reap the mental and physical benefits.

Similarly, E. O. Wilson's *Biophilia Hypothesis* suggests that we may have evolved preferences for other living things and natural environments. Which do you prefer: the concrete, asphalt, and metal of a big city or the colorful cliffs and leaves of your favorite crag? Okay, that was a biased question.

Intrinsic/Extrinsic Motivation Theory emphasizes the fact that sometimes we are motivated for internal reasons, other times for external reasons. Intrinsic motives include enjoying the activity for its own sake, interest, and a desire to overcome challenge or master a skill just for your own satisfaction. Extrinsic motives include money, grades, awards, recognition, and fame. Therefore, extrinsic motivation is often associated with competition. People differ in their tendencies to be intrinsically versus extrinsically motivated. "I'm only doing this for the paycheck" versus "I would do this without pay or reward, when no one else is around." The highest levels of motivation and performance are likely to occur when we are motivated both intrinsically and extrinsically.

Applied to climbing, intrinsic motives would include the joy of moving over stone, the beauty of the crags and good routes, the natural setting, as well as a desire to get better just for the sake of mastery. The latter is referred to as *mastery motivation* and is associated with intrinsic motivation. In contrast, a primary concern with outcomes is called *performance motivation* and is associated with extrinsic motivation and competition, formal or informal.

As prototypical examples in climbing, contrast the following climbers. Climber A is bouldering all alone on unnamed, ungraded problems. She is enjoying her surroundings, the sun, the problem-solving, the moves, the feel of her muscles working hard, and the sense that she is improving. Climber B feels compelled to climb cutting-edge routes in popular areas so that his achievements will be noted by other climbers, as well as his sponsors. If it weren't for competition, his prowess, and recognition, he wouldn't bother climbing. Clearly, Climber A is more intrinsically motivated and Climber B is more extrinsically motivated.

Although higher levels of performance are often achieved when both forms of motivation are present, we can contrast extreme cases like Climber A and Climber B who are almost exclusively motivated by one or the other form. Intrinsically motivated climbers with mastery motivation are likely to learn more, have more fun, persist longer, and achieve more. Because they enjoy climbing, training doesn't seem like a burden. Because they have a mastery motivation, they want to learn, not just show off. They are more likely to choose routes that appeal to them regardless of ratings and often become lifelong climbers. Extrinsically motivated climbers are more likely to choose a route or competition that will allow their accomplishments to be recognized, rather than one that will be fun or maximize their learning. Ratings matter more to them. If they experience a plateau or injury, they may quit. If external incentives (e.g., sponsorship, comp rankings) are removed, they may quit.

A person's balance between intrinsic and extrinsic motives fluctuates over time. Ironically, we can be "punished by rewards" when sponsors, coaches, or parents motivate us by dangling those carrots in front of us. As extrinsic motivation is promoted, intrinsic motivation may dwindle, spoiling the experience. Part of the problem is we feel like we have less control over our choices. We feel like we have to climb. Climbing becomes a j-o-b. Picture the kids who love to play pick-up games of basketball with their friends when they are young but lose their passion in college when forced to practice or else be threatened with losing their scholarships. Similarly, picture the kids who love to climb, and fall, and swing on the rope—until their parents snidely tell them they can't use the blue holds or shouldn't be swinging.

Competence Motivation Theory and *Achievement Motivation Theory* focus on what is believed to be an innate or instinctual desire to achieve success and avoid failure. People with a higher need for achievement may feel an internal sense of reward when successful and be less concerned with external rewards. People develop a tendency toward competence motivation during childhood due to approval or disapproval they experience when attempting to master new tasks. Positive feelings (e.g., joy, pride) are associated with competence and negative feelings (e.g., shame, embarrassment, anxiety) are associated with failure and poor performances. As a result, children and adults tend to be drawn toward activities in which they perceive themselves as competent and repelled by activities where they expect failure.

Applied to climbing, competence and achievement may come in very small or very large forms. We may be rewarded with feelings of competence when we:

- do a move with style
- finally get a hard move we have been attempting
- learn a new technique
- send a project
- onsight some goal route
- climb at a new level
- overcome doubts or fear

The opportunities for those of us who have a high need for achievement are endless. There is always another route or problem to challenge us.

Affect Theory focuses on the affective (i.e., emotional) payoffs and punishments that motivate us. Note the term affect is roughly equivalent to emotion. We are driven to maximize positive emotions (e.g., interest, excitement, joy, pride) and minimize negative emotions (e.g., boredom, sadness, fear). Affect theory doesn't contradict the other theories; it focuses attention on what is believed to underlie all the rest—emotion. Emotions are viewed as evolutionary adaptations. They lend the force or motivational impulse to other adaptations. For example, emotions distinguish a boring meal from a culinary "experience." They are the bottom-line reason we seek competence, avoid failure, and fear falling. Shame and embarrassment play a central role in fear of failure (Chapters 7-9).

Applied to climbing, a good day is when the balance tips toward positive emotions and a bad day is when the balance tips the other direction. We don't enjoy frustration and fear, but the pride and competence we experience at overcoming challenge and fear outweigh them.

Why Do <u>You</u> Climb?

If you want climbing to be more enjoyable and possibly improve performance, then consider your motives, priorities, and goals. Why do you climb? What do you get out of it? What do you want out of it? Which of the theories and factors that we discussed best describe your motivations? We often know we are motivated to do something without explicitly identifying why. However, putting motives in words can help you reveal their pros and cons—hidden payoffs and traps. Try to be honest with yourself. You can write your answers here or elsewhere if that helps you to be more honest:

- To what degree is your climbing motivated by arousal/ seeking to escape boredom?
  _____
  _____

- To what degree does climbing just feel natural?
  _____
  _____

- To what degree are you motivated to be in natural environments?
  _____
  _____

- What are your intrinsic motives?
  _____
  _____

- What are your extrinsic motives?
  _____
  _____

- To what degree are you motivated by feelings of competence? _____

- Is your need for achievement low or high?

- Perhaps most importantly, are you more motivated to achieve success or avoid failure?

- Given your answers above, which motives are most powerful? What are your major sources of motivation?

If you are really interested in these ideas and want a better self-assessment, questionnaires exist to assess most of these principles of motivation. For example, you can easily assess your need for achievement.

Regardless of your answers now, you will probably find new insights into your own motives as we discuss topics related to these theories in later chapters. You may want to re-visit your answers after you have finished this book. More importantly, you may want to modify some of your scripts to maximize your positive motives (those that increase performance and make your climbing more fun) and minimize your negative motives (those that hold you back and spoil your fun).

Too Much Motivation?

All this talk of motivation raises the question: Can we ever be too motivated? Perhaps. If your motivation to train drives you to injury, then your motivation exceeded your physical capacity to endure that volume of training. This is a common problem for motivated beginners who build muscle more quickly than they can strengthen connective tissue. It is also a problem for experienced climbers who overemphasize performance motivation, leading them to chase numbers in spite of overuse injuries.

Similarly, if your motivation to climb drives you to neglect other important aspects of your life, you may end up unhappy later on. Although all of these problems can be attributed to too much motivation, they could equally be attributed to the wrong kinds of motivation. For example, extrinsic motivation is more likely to lead to over-training because we focus on short-term recognition or reward in contrast to long-term gains that require us to stay healthy. Extreme weight loss is another example of this tradeoff.

As with extrinsic motivation, competence motivation is wonderful in moderation. However, if your only sense of competence and pride comes from climbing performance, you are setting yourself up for disappointment. You will be more likely to put counter-productive levels of pressure on yourself, over-train, and get injured. And what happens to your self-worth when you eventually stop progressing or do get injured? You may have nothing to fall back on.

Sensation-Seeking Personality

Personality theory offers another type of explanation for why we enjoy climbing and are motivated to dedicate ourselves to the climbing lifestyle. Specifically, the *sensation-seeking personality* describes a sub-group of people who find novelty, complexity, intensity, excitement, and even fear particularly rewarding. "Risk-taker" is sometimes used as a synonym—or pejorative term by folks who disapprove. However, risk is not necessary or essential. For example, sensation-seekers enjoy traveling to new places and eating unusual or intense foods. Psychologists have pointed out that risk is not the focus; risk is the price sensation-seekers pay to fight boredom.

Sensation-seeking should sound familiar because it relates to the optimal arousal discussed earlier in this chapter. Interestingly, the subtitle of Marvin Zuckerman's 1979 book on sensation-seeking is *Beyond Optimal Level of Arousal*. Whereas the latter theory applies to everyone, in that we all have an optimal level, sensation-seeking applies to a specific group of people who require "more" to reach their optimal level.

Research supports the assertion that sensation-seekers are physiologically different. They tend to differ from non-seekers in levels of certain neurotransmitters. Neurotransmitters are the chemical messengers that relay signals between neurons in your brain. Dopamine is a neurotransmitter associated with pleasure and reward. It helps us identify rewards, motivates us to seek them, and makes them feel more pleasurable. Sensation-seekers are more likely to have a different dopamine receptor gene. Similarly, MAO (monoamine oxidase) regulates dopamine. Sensation-seekers tend to have lower levels of MAO. Less MAO means more dopamine/more pleasure. Adrenalin has also been implicated in the development of sensation-seeking. Of course, we are all familiar with the term "adrenalin addict."

These biologically-based personality differences manifest in a variety of ways. Zuckerman developed the readily available Sensation Seeking Scale in order to identify and study sensation-seekers. Its subscales illustrate the various ways arousal may be pursued:

- Thrill and Adventure Seeking: extreme sports; speed, danger...
- Disinhibition: social stimulation; parties, sex, rock n' roll...
- Experience-Seeking: mental and sense stimulation; unusual lifestyles, travel, foods, drugs...
- Boredom Susceptibility: dislike of routine, repetition, dull people...

The first subscale, Thrill and Adventure Seeking, most obviously applies to climbing. In fact, the Sensation Seeking Scale includes an item that says: "I often wish I could be a mountain climber." Cute, huh? However, the subscales tend to correlate, and it's not hard to observe this among climbers. Many dislike routine. Many enjoy travel and unusual foods. Drugs? You decide. Unusual lifestyle? Anyone who has road-tripped or, better yet been a climbing bum, understands that connection. When we say they are correlated, that means they tend to occur together in people, but not always. In all likelihood, some of those subscales probably describe you more than others.

The bottom-line answer for why we enjoy climbing so much may just be because we are wired differently!

Other Payoffs

The neurotransmitters we discussed in relation to the sensation-seeking personality aren't the only ones that apply to climbing. The endorphin rush refers to the pleasure we feel in the midst of exercise, excitement, danger, or pain. The rush is no surprise given that the name endorphin comes from endo (endogenous) and orphin (morphine). Basically, an endorphin is a natural morphine, which reduces our perception of pain and produces a high. That pain reduction can come in handy when your forearms are pumped beyond belief or your fingers and toes are crunched in a crack.

The terms rush, high, and morphine point to the addictive side of climbing. In climbing addiction, they are combined with intermittent reinforcement, meaning you have to keep trying, not knowing when that big payoff (e.g., onsight, redpoint, flow) will come. Intermittent reinforcement explains why kids whose parents give-in learn to whine persistently, and why gambling is so addictive. Climbing presents us with endless opportunities to chase the flow, the high, the rush. And success is never guaranteed. Add in all the other wonderful payoffs we gain through climbing and it is no surprise so many of us are addicted.

Stumbling on Happiness

Sometimes we just don't know what will make us happy. We believe that if X or Y happens, then we will be happy or miserable. However, we are pretty bad with these predictions. Harvard psychologist Dan Gilbert has researched this problem, which he refers to as *affective forecasting*. Affective forecasting is predicting our emotional reactions to future events. The title of his book *Stumbling on Happiness* is meant to be a double pun. The first pun captures the following problem. We often think we know what will make us happy, so we chase that dream only to find that it isn't as great as we had expected once we achieve it. We "stumbled" because we chased the wrong dream. The second pun is that we sometime accidentally "stumble" into situations that make us happy. We didn't expect it and wouldn't have predicted it but, "Hey, this is pretty darn good."

Similarly, we often overestimate the misery we will feel if bad things come to pass. Why are we so bad at knowing how we will feel? Gilbert has discovered a number of reasons. For example, when it comes to bad events, we underestimate the power of our "psychological immune system." The latter refers to our ability to bounce back. We often find a silver lining in a bad situation. We often find ways to rationalize bad outcomes. When it comes to good events, we often habituate. A new job, falling in love, sending your first 5.13 all bring happiness, but habituation means we get used to the new situation and the intensity fades.

When I was at the height of my climbing addiction, I enjoyed the success of a hard won redpoint for mere hours. My joy was short-lived because I immediately jumped on a new project, only to have my ass kicked all over again.

Another huge limitation in predicting our happiness is the fact that we are usually pursuing something we have not experienced before. The problem is that because we haven't experienced it firsthand, we don't know the downsides. *Stumbling* is not a self-help book; however, understanding Gilbert's research can help us avoid some mistakes. One of his suggestions is based on the discrepancy he finds between "forecasters" who predict how they will feel if X happens and "experiencers" who report how they actually feel while X is happening. Experiencers are there— where we think we want to be.

As an example, many of us think that becoming a sponsored elite climber would be the greatest thing in the world. We are merely forecasters. We are unlikely to fully appreciate the downsides of achieving that dream. Experiencers are the actual sponsored elite climbers. Is their experience overwhelmingly positive? I doubt it. As we discussed under extrinsic motivation, climbing becomes a j-o-b. There is pressure to perform, the threat of injury, the threat of losing sponsorship, and the ever-present awareness that sponsorship won't last forever. Moreover, fame brings expectations: "Oh my god, Joe Blow fell off a mere 5.13!" Fame also brings jealousy, criticism, and rumors. Fred Rouhling's ascent of Akira in 1995 still makes the news because he claimed it was the world's first 9b and other climbers didn't believe he had actually climbed it. A recent Climbing Magazine article documented the controversy. Top climbers still criticize Rouhling.

If you doubt the power of these drawbacks, consider a situation that seems even more clearly ideal: winning a multi-million-dollar lottery. The happiness of lottery winners has been studied. They are typically very happy for six months to a year. Then many of them return to their base level of happiness. The pros are balanced by cons that most of us wouldn't expect: poor investment decisions, begging relatives and neighbors, letters and phone calls from strangers, threats, and jealous friends. Many winners end up feeling socially isolated.

Another problem in our affective forecasting is that we often get focused on "that one thing" that will change everything for us. We tend to overlook all the things that will stay the same: chores, injuries, bad weather, annoying colleagues and family members…

The implications for climbing are several:

- Don't put all your eggs in one happiness basket. If you want to climb at a high level, you have to focus on goals. However, that one special redpoint is unlikely to change your life. Pursue multiple goals, some more easily attainable than others. Beyond climbing, find balance in life. Hopefully there are other things to enjoy and other achievements to feel proud of.

- Experiment. Try other types of climbing. I often hear trad climbers diss sport climbing ("Sport climbing is neither."). Even though Don and I were originally trads who started well before sport climbing existed, we can't understand this blanket rejection of sport climbing. You might be surprised when you stumble on happiness with a new type of climbing, a new area, or a new partner.

- Related to the previous point, variety is good. First, we are less likely to habituate to the happiness that the same old thing brings us. Second, we are less likely to stagnate in terms of motivation and learning.

- Repeat what works, meaning what brings you happiness. That sounds like a contradiction to the last two points but there is a caveat. If you don't experience that situation too often, you won't habituate to it, the joy won't wear off. Gilbert's example is fine dining. If you eat the same wonderful meal every night, it becomes less wonderful. However, if you eat it once a month, it maintains its appeal. In Chapter 10, we talk about flow. We are unlikely to habituate to flow experiences because they are all too rare, and they involve variety and novelty.

- Research your goals. Talk to experiencers. What's it like to live in Rifle or Yosemite for months at a time? What's it like to be a pro? What are the pros and cons of hanging that campus board in your basement?

Lessons from the Aged

"I haven't missed a swell in 55 years. . . . I'm still as excited about surfing as I've ever been. I mean I literally run to the water with my board, hooting and laughing and giggling."
– Mickey Munoz, surfing pioneer and board shaper

In the last few years I've noticed a theme repeated in conversations with older climbers like myself. We are having more fun now than when we were younger. Most of us were climbing harder 10 or 20 years ago—maybe by a little, maybe by a lot—but that doesn't seem to diminish this recurring sentiment. Contrast the old geezer (maybe I exaggerate) dangling at the end of the rope, having a great time after falling on his redpoint attempt of a 12+ (or 11+, 10+,…) with a much younger climber throwing a wobbler after falling off a 5.14. What's the difference besides age and grade? Most likely their goals and motives differ substantially.

So, why are these "old-timers" enjoying climbing more now? Some reasons we have heard and said ourselves:

- Intrinsic motivation: More of our drive to climb comes from the intrinsic motivation discussed earlier in the chapter. It may have been a motivator all along, but now it accounts for a greater percentage of our motivation. We are at the crags to enjoy the experience, the movement, the rock, the natural setting, and friends.
- Extrinsic motivation: Intrinsic and extrinsic motivation are not necessarily inversely related, but for most of us older climbers, the greater percentage of intrinsic motivation may be due to extrinsic motivation decreasing. It is unlikely that we are motivated by dreams of fame, glory, or sponsorship.

- Different expectations: We still love to be in shape and climb hard but we don't expect to set new personal bests.
- Identity: We have come to realize that being a climber is just one part of our identities. We have been through cycles of being in and out of shape due to injuries, children, work, and unexpected life events. If we can't climb, it's disappointing but not devastating. We still have value.
- Perspective: We know climbing is awesome. That's why we are still doing it after so many years. But once again, we've dealt with injuries and deaths, had children, and faced unexpected life events. As a result, we've come to realize that there are more important things in life than climbing.
- Patience: Given our comments about "identity" and "perspective," we have greater patience, which means less frustration. We are more likely to take things in stride when we are forced to miss a workout or a climbing trip.
- Less fear of failure: Fear of failure is discussed in great detail in Chapters 7 and 8, but at its core is concern over how others evaluate us. We just don't care as much as we used to, for a number of reasons. We may have lower expectations for ourselves and other people most likely have lower expectations of us. We have experienced more years of "failures" or sub-par performances. We realize there are more important things in life than climbing and that climbing is just one part of our identities. Therefore, "failure" doesn't present the same threat to us.
- Less social comparison: Comparing ourselves to others is linked to fear of failure. Social comparison tends to make people unhappy in the long-term, even if they generally compare favorably. Older climbers are less likely to buy into this dangerous game. Then again, there aren't

that many of us out there and we rarely feel compelled to compare ourselves to much younger climbers.

- Generativity: Generativity is a term used by the brilliant developmental psychologist Erik Erikson to describe the desire of middle-aged and older individuals to give back to their community. They may volunteer to help other people, especially younger generations. In climbing, this often takes the form of helping younger climbers get to the crags, coaching, or new route development. Through the latter, older climbers can make contributions that will last for many years and be enjoyed by thousands of climbers.

- Priorities: We thought we should "book-end" this list by starting with Intrinsic Motivation and ending with Priorities because they are intimately related. Our high intrinsic motivation is often evident in our priorities: Have fun and stay healthy (including injury-free).

Many of the items on this list will be discussed in Chapters 7 and 8 on fear of failure. Those chapters will further explain the dynamics and definitions of these topics. Interestingly, the trend toward more fun and greater subjective well-being later in our climbing careers is consistent with research on aging. In general, well-being stays pretty constant over the lifespan and many older people enjoy greater well-being. Some of the same factors are at work: expectations, identity, goals, perspective, and patience.

Another explanation for why older climbers seem to have more fun is selection bias. Selection bias occurs in research when we choose a sample that isn't representative of everyone else. One reason for selection bias is "mortality"—not that a lot of climbers are dying, rather the climbers who loved it stayed with it. The ones who didn't love it, dropped out, creating "mortality" in the research sense. Climbers who were ambivalent about climbing eventually quit or drifted away from climbing. Therefore, bias in our sample could exist because older people who are still climbing may be different than older people who quit climbing. In what ways?

- We may have been more intrinsically motivated all along. Extrinsically motivated athletes are more likely to quit when those external motivators go away. Once scholarships, awards, prizes, and recognition are in the past, extrinsically motivated people have little reason to continue.

- We may have been less driven by performance or competition all along. It's not hard to read old climbing magazines or competition results in order to find "flash-in-the-pan" climbers. By this we mean climbers who progressed rapidly to top levels and then suddenly gave it up. Some of them quit when they faced their first plateau or injury. (See "Patience" in the previous list.)

- A third reason has to do with personal history with sports. While researching his book *50 Athletes Over 50*, Don identified three groups of older athletes: Groovers, Bloomers, and Innovators. Groovers have done the same sport for almost their whole life but they are in the minority. Bloomers pick up sports later in life. Innovators, the largest group by far, switch from sport to sport in order to adapt to changes in their situation (e.g., injuries, availability of facilities). Groovers just love their sport and can't imagine life without it. Most are highly intrinsically motivated. So, these are the older climbers who have been climbing for decades and bias our sample with their enthusiasm. Bloomers got inspired by some event late in their life that turned them into athletes. They may be intrinsically motivated to exercise in general. Innovators love being fit and healthy and adapt what they do so that they can stay active. In addition to intrinsic motivation, many are driven by the optimal arousal and novelty seeking we discussed. Bloomers and Innovators are less likely to have been climbing for decades, by definition, but they are all likely to show passion.

A Self-Study of Fun

Don and I realized we have learned a lot of lessons over the years about how to shape our climbing experiences. Our performance levels have fluctuated, but perhaps more importantly, our levels of enjoyment have fluctuated. The causes of these fluctuations and associated lessons directly involve psychological concepts discussed in this chapter and future chapters.

We enjoy climbing the most when we:
- climb with good friends.
- climb in new areas or climb new routes.
- pick routes for their quality as opposed to grade.
- pick areas for their beauty or great weather.
- keep climbing in perspective and balance it with the rest of our lives.
- focus on the process of climbing and learning, rather than the outcome.
- take in the whole experience, not just the tick list.
- experience flow

And when we don't:
- over-identify with climbing.
- worry about what other people think.
- over-train or get injured!

Exercises

You can write your answers here or elsewhere if that helps you to be more honest:

- What aspects of climbing or types of climbing do you enjoy most?

  _____

  _____

- What aspects of climbing do you enjoy least?

  _____

  _____

- Given the answers above, can you change climbing to be even more rewarding?

  _____

- Who are you? What is your identity—as a climber and beyond?

  _____

  _____

- Who do you most enjoy climbing with? Why?

  _____

  _____

- So, who should you try to be like?

  _____

  _____

In this chapter, we explored the question of why we climb. We surveyed psychological theories of motivation and emotions that directly apply to climbing. By now it should be obvious that the answers to why we climb are many, varied, and complex. Moreover, they are personal. Your reasons probably differ from mine. Socrates said "The unexamined life is not worth living." Although that may be a bit of an exaggeration, we would agree that the unexamined climbing life is probably less enjoyable and leads to lower performance. Examining why we do what we do, our motives, and what makes us happy, opens opportunities to maximize enjoyment and performance. We also firmly believe that enjoyment and performance are not inherently correlated. We can work hard to climb at high levels while having fun. At the same time, climbing at high levels in no way guarantees fun, if you put too much pressure on yourself or climb for the wrong reasons.

In the next chapter, we examine fear from a psychological and physiological perspective. That sets the stage for later chapters where we deal with fear of falling and fear of failure. These fears may do the opposite of everything we discussed in this chapter. They may hold us back, demotivate us, and detract from our enjoyment of climbing.

Fear and Performance

By Jeff Elison and Don McGrath

> **The only thing we have to fear is fear itself.**
> – *Franklin D. Roosevelt*

The Fear-Gravity Parallel

We need physical strength to overcome the forces that gravity exerts on our bodies as we climb. We push and pull upward against gravity's constant force. The stronger our arms, legs, and core, the better we can overcome the gravitational pull. If it is gravity that we are working against physically, what force are we working against mentally? It certainly isn't gravity. The force that we work against with our mental strength is fear. Fear, like gravity, is ever-present so we fight it constantly.

Whereas gravity exerts its force in one direction, fear comes in many forms: fear of falling, fear of pain, and fear of failure. More importantly, these fears are not as simple to understand as gravity. In addition, I am using the term fear as many psychologists do to include nervousness, anxiety, panic, desperation, terror, etc. Especially in the more mild forms, we may not even be conscious of their effects. For example, we say we fell because we were pumped or weren't strong enough. But the real problem may have been fear causing us to hesitate or overgrip. Similarly, we decide to repeat a route, rather than face a new challenge. Why? Perhaps we are afraid we might flail in front of other climbers. Therefore, fear deserves some study so that we can understand it and learn to manage it to our advantage.

In physical training, we train our muscles and nervous system so that we can successfully overcome the force of gravity. We strengthen our fingers, arms, legs, and core to develop contact strength, delay forearm pump, and maximize lock-off power. We practice technique to learn movements and execute them smoothly. Just as we target these multiple elements of physical conditioning, the following chapters will target multiple elements of our mental game. To achieve physical gains and overcome gravity's force, we employ a wide variety of training methods. Therefore, overcoming the more complex forces of fear requires the innovative and varied methods of mental training that we will describe in this and following chapters.

Perspectives on Fear

Fear is a central topic in this book, encompassing fear in many forms. Therefore, before we deal with specific fears, it is worth a few paragraphs to step back and get a broader perspective on fear. Fear is an evolutionary adaptation that humans share with all mammals and many, many much older species. Why? Because it helps keep us alive and intact (allowing the opportunity for sex and reproduction). Clearly, fear can be a good thing. Obviously, it can be bad as well. Evolution has dealt with these kinds of tradeoffs between pros and cons for hundreds of millions of years—and fear is still with us. Therefore, the pros must outweigh the cons, overall. So, let's take a look at the good and bad sides of fear. Understanding both the pros and cons will help us take control of fear, allow us to take advantage of it, optimize our fear, with the end result being improved performance. (And we do mean "optimize" as you will see.)

Fear readies our bodies for fight or flight. On the plus side, the fight mechanism can help us while climbing. Adrenalin gets released, blood glucose increases, heart rate and blood pressure increase, digestion slows, and attention increases. In many cases, fear allows us to fight through the tough sections. On the down side, the fight mechanism may be dialed up too high. We become too tense, breathe poorly, overgrip, waste energy, experience tunnel vision—we fail. Another down side is that the flight mechanism may cause us to freeze up, grab a draw, or take—rather than move upward toward success. The latter is like a deer frozen in car headlights.

The Whippers Effect

Most importantly for this book, the fight or flight mechanism affects our brains and thinking, as well. It changes attention and focus. At mild-to-moderate levels, fear helps us focus, helps us pay attention and, as a result, increases working memory (short-term memory). At these helpful levels, we often have a broader focus of attention—we can take in more information from a variety of sources (holds, options, protection, fall potential, safety). Remember that working memory is where conscious thinking and problem solving occur. The boost to attention and working memory means we think better and have enhanced problem-solving abilities. And that's what onsighting is all about. The end result is increased performance; we perceive, think, and remember more clearly. Think about the vivid memories you get from some (but not all) scary experiences. Think about the moments of flow when everything just clicked—you saw the options and reacted almost instinctively. It's not that you were without anxiety; you just weren't consumed by it.

On the down side, those attentional effects may backfire at high levels of fear. When fear is too intense, we get tunnel vision. We can only focus on one or two things, and working memory is consumed by them. We lose the ability to process a wide variety of informational sources. We can't even see all the holds, all the options. Higher-level thinking and problem solving are out the window. Think about the seconds before your last big fall while onsighting. Your mind was probably racing, everything seemed to happen very quickly, and suddenly you were at the end of the rope. No memory of details.

These attentional effects make sense from an evolutionary perspective. Low levels of fear usually occur in response to non-specific threats (a dark forest, a job interview). High levels of fear usually occur in response to specific threats (a rattle-snake, a thief with a gun). In both cases, we want our attention to be boosted. We don't want to be ignoring threats or relevant information. In the case of the forest, we are sensitized to any stimulus. We want to pay attention to anything and everything that moves or growls. That's why the startle response is "potentiated"—we jump at the drop of a pin. Conversely, in the case of the rattlesnake, nothing is more important, so we tunnel in on it. Memory follows attention and the tunnel vision we get shows up in what forensic psychologists call the "weapons effect." This is the tendency for witnesses of crimes involving weapons to remember the weapon—and not much else. For climbers we could call this the *Whippers Effect*.

The Whippers Effect occurs in climbing when real or imagined fears focus our attention to the point of tunnel vision. We may be thinking about the fall, seeing only our hands groping for the next hold, ignoring footholds, technique, and proper breathing. After we fall, we have little memory about what just occurred because we were too focused to attend to other aspects of the situation. That's why fear can have negative effects on learning.

The Whippers Effect is one reason why our drills suggest practicing new scripts under safe conditions, such as top-roping. The effect also has implications for learning redpoint beta. Stick clipping the bolt above you or top-roping from the anchor allows you to hang at each section, inspect the holds, and remember under low-fear conditions. Many of us have been on routes where you have to do a hard move 10' above a bolt. You get there pumped, try to work it out, but you only have seconds before you take the whip. Tunnel vision and the limited time make it extremely difficult to work out and memorize the beta. Rehearsing while safe is much more effective and efficient. Plus a top-rope conserves energy and skin since you don't have to re-climb as much or yard back up. This increases the number of attempts you can make.

The Performance-Arousal Curve

The hell of these tradeoffs in physiological and mental effects is that they coincide. In other words, when your body is too amped, you are probably experiencing tunnel vision too. And on the bright side, at moderate levels both the physio and mental effects are in your favor. These observations have been captured in the well-known Performance-Arousal Curve (Figure 4.1). This graph of the relationship between performance and arousal is often described as an inverse-U. Let's work from left-to-right to see its implications.

At the far left, where arousal is low and anxiety is non-existent, we are experiencing boredom and disinterest. Obviously, if we are bored, we are neither paying attention nor motivated to perform well. Think about a time when you were forced to play a board game that you hate. You probably had a tough time staying awake, much less competing. Moving a bit to the right, we start to get interested, and as a result, physiological arousal, attention, motivation, and performance increase. So, now maybe it's a board game you kind of like. Moving right farther, interest turns to excitement; physiological effects, attention, motivation, and performance rise, possibly peaking. If not, then they probably peak with low-to-moderate levels of anxiety or fear. (Where the peak occurs depends on factors we will soon discuss.) Now we are talking about a favorite game where you want to trounce that poser new-guy.

Move farther right and we see that with too much fear everything goes downhill, literally. We are on the wrong side of the curve. Your heart pounds, hands sweat, muscles clench. Attention is either tunneled or scattered all over the place. Working memory just isn't working. Performance tanks. In fact, some research using Catastrophe Theory to model performance suggests this curve isn't so pleasantly smooth. Rather, the drop off may be precipitous—a term all climbers can appreciate. The line between the peak and choking may be very abrupt. Let's not go there—or let's minimize how often we do.

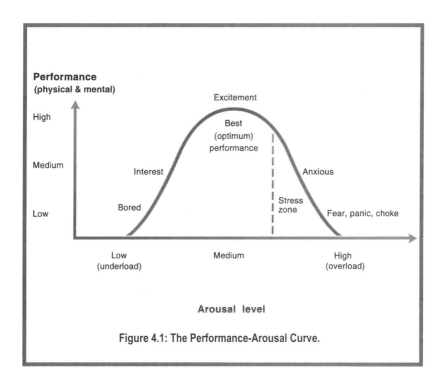

Figure 4.1: The Performance-Arousal Curve.

There are several take-away points to be had from this analysis. First, fear isn't all bad—we shouldn't unilaterally fear it. Second, there are optimal levels of fear. (We use the plural "levels" intentionally because which level is optimal depends on those yet-to-be-discussed factors). Third, understanding the curve can help us control fear to find those optimal levels. Fourth, we have some control over where we sit on the curve— and, thus, how we perform.

Factors Affecting the Performance-Arousal Relationship

Let's take a look at those factors that affect optimal levels of arousal. The most widely researched factor is "task difficulty." Difficulty here refers to intricate skill versus brute force. Contrast thc small-muscle, fine, precise motor movements required for that precision deadpoint from slopers to a letterbox versus the large muscle thuggish body-length dyno from ledge to ledge. High levels of anxiety and muscle tension aren't going to allow the precision you need to hit that letterbox, so the curve shifts to the left. You experience peak performance at lower levels of arousal and even modest levels of fear may cause you to choke. In contrast, chugging Red Bull, beating your chest, and primal screaming may optimize your chances at that body-length dyno. It's hard to be too amped in such a situation.

So, great, another variable. What does this mean for your projects? It gives you another tactic, another way to size them up. It gives you the flexibility to adjust your approach to the specifics of your situation. Do you need to amp yourself up or dial it down? You may adjust per route, but sometimes per section. During an onsight, you need to conserve energy, take in every hold and option, let working memory flow, and make quick decisions on the spot. But even during onsights, you may hit the moment of truth where you just have to bear down and crank. During redpoints, you also have times at which you conserve energy versus times when you crank. Moreover, you know the route, so you may get an overall feel for whether you need to play it cool (long-enduro or delicate precision routes) versus amp up (the 3-bolt powerfest).

A second variable that affects the optimal level of arousal is you! There are individual differences in the way our bodies and brains react to anxiety and arousal. Some of us perform better at higher levels and some of us at lower levels. Red Bull works for some of us and against others. You can get a sense for this by monitoring how you react to stress in your life, in general. Better yet, be specific and analyze how your level of arousal affects your climbing.

How do you typically react when facing a stressful situation on a climb? In the spaces below, note one or two specific instances and how you reacted.

_____

_____

_____

_____

A third variable, related to the previous point, is your perception of fear and your perception of your own body's reactions. For example, anxiety makes our hearts speed up and our hands sweat (measurable with GSR technology at levels so low we can't even perceive the changes). So, how do you react when you do perceive these reactions? It could be anywhere from "Great" to "Oh no, I'm losing control," literally. For example, panic attacks are a diagnosable psychological condition. Some event or thought triggers a person's fear and their fear spirals out of control. And so do they. They may fear they are having a heart attack or some other physical problem. Some sufferers end up in the emergency room. One large contributor to panic attacks is the perception or interpretation of the bodily reactions to normal stress. They say: "Oh no, my heart is racing, my chest is constricting, my palms and face are sweating." These thoughts lead to misguided interpretations: "I must be having a heart attack" or "I'm going to make a fool of myself in public." Their interpretations lead to more fear, which lead to more intense symptoms, which lead to more fear.... You get the idea.

Irrational? Yes, but understandable. First, these events become scripted. If people do worry themselves into being sick or making a scene, then they come to expect it to happen again—a script. Second, under conditions of intense fear, few of us are rational. Remember those effects on attention and working memory we discussed. It becomes hard to pay attention to anything else, to distract yourself, and harder to think clearly.

We're not suggesting that many climbers suffer from full-blown panic attacks. If you did, you probably wouldn't be a climber. The point is that our perceptions and interpretations of our bodily symptoms vary and form a feedback loop that can be detrimental. Or the loop can be broken and performance increased. So, how do we adjust our interpretations? As we've seen before, scripts rely on beliefs (rational or irrational) and interpretations are simply one category of beliefs.

ABC's in Action

Modifying maladaptive interpretations provides an ideal example of the ABC process. In the extreme, choking (or failure) is the undesirable Consequence in this example. The initial Antecedent may be some climb or situation, but let's fast-forward to the point where we perceive bodily effects of anxiety and treat those as the immediate Antecedent. (We can and will move backward, chaining these events together to address fear and bodily effects as unwanted Consequences). Irrational Beliefs that commonly lie between physical symptoms and subsequent choking include: "These symptoms are going to get worse," "I'm going to lose control," or simply "I can't do this; my performance will suck." Now that we have the ABC sequence and some B's to work with, let's start debunking/questioning them. What evidence do we have for and against these beliefs?

First, being all logical and scientific, refer back to the Performance-Arousal Curve for counterevidence. Science tells us that being under-aroused is a bad thing, bad for performance. So, maybe your anxiety is a good thing. Praise Science!

Second, make science personal. Have you ever felt like this and performed well? Unless your fear is really intense, I'm guessing you have. I don't know your personal experiences, so I'll give you my favorite example and hope you can relate: job interviews. I can remember my first interviews as a high school student and new college graduate. I was nervous and my nervousness distracted me. I didn't do my best, but they worked out. I got an offer for almost every job for which I interviewed. This allowed me to form a new script, reinterpret my anxiety, and improve my performance in future interviews. I was able to tell myself that my racing heart and sweaty hands were part of performance-enhancing anxiety. It even allowed me to say, "Interviewers are used to clammy hands, so don't worry about shaking hands." In fact, now I can take 90% of those bodily effects and either ignore them or leverage them, knowing they lead to better performance. This frees up my attention and working memory for the problem at hand: interpreting questions, reactions, and coming up with the best response. On a good day, climbing is just like that. I'm amped for the route, try to adjust my level of amped-ness, and use it to my advantage. It's like FDR said, "The only thing we have to fear is fear itself."

Third, look for evidence. How often have you choked due to anxiety? If you are very lucky the answer is never. More likely, the answer is rarely. However, as climbers, some of us put ourselves in potentially choke-inducing situations far more than other folks. If the answer is frequently, then we sure hope these suggestions can help you re-write your scripts to be more effective. And maybe the next point will make that easier.

Fourth, question the losing control aspect. Arousal often rises to the appropriate level—the level at which you need to be—and doesn't' continue to the downhill part of the curve. The appropriate level may even be a bit of anxiety. If you don't let fear spiral, if you don't misinterpret sensations, if you believe in optimal arousal, then you can keep fear under control. We're not saying you can eliminate fear in all circumstances, nor would you want to. However, with knowledge and practice, you can gain greater control over your fear and increase your performance.

Hopefully, these examples illustrate the importance of fear perception and interpretation of bodily reactions. We can magnify the significance of accelerated hearts and clammy palms and end up in the downward-spiral-to-choke or we can make fear our ally and optimize our performances.

Uncertainty and Fear

Other variables affect fear and thus performance. Evolution has hard-wired us with regard to novelty, change, the unfamiliar, and uncertainty. Low-to-moderate levels of these are interesting or even exciting. As an example, think about dating. There is so much novelty, mystery, and interest during the early days of a relationship. However, high levels of any of these trigger fear. That is one of the major reasons why onsighting is so much harder than redpointing. It's not just that you haven't practiced the moves. A major challenge is the unknown. Fear and anxiety are common experiences when you don't know what's coming next. Is that a jug or a sloper? Will I be able to clip that next bolt? Onsighting takes major mind control to ensure that fear and doubts don't distract from your focus, detract from your ability to process the ever-changing information, and cause you to waste energy. You have to stay relaxed and mentally open. On the other hand, redpointing takes a somewhat different sort of mind control. You know it's hard. You've taken those falls. You may have felt like you'll never get it. And you have to mentally overcome all those thoughts. I will discuss frustration and failure in Chapters 7 and 8.

Most climbers find redpointing easier than onsighting due to the inherent uncertainty in the latter. In addition, redpointing allows you to overlearn moves, creating automaticity. In Chapter 2, I mentioned that overlearning reduces anxiety and choking. Thus, lower levels of uncertainty and the opportunity to over-learn moves explain why we typically see a full number-grade difference in most climbers' achievement between their best on-sight and best redpoint. In fact, this rule of thumb is apparent when we look at which climbers are "good onsighters" versus "good redpointers." Climbers who are better at onsighting have a smaller difference, perhaps two letter grades. Redpoint special-ists (or weak onsighters depending on your perspective) may have a gap of six to eight letter grades. In most cases, the size of this difference is due to practice and scripting. People who have a small difference between their levels of performance are prob-ably more comfortable with uncertainty, have better mind con-trol for those particular challenges, and have better scripts for self-control—all due to practice. We bet they attempt onsights more often, too. We're not saying that's better. We're just pointing out that we get comfortable with, and develop better scripts for, whatever it is we practice. On the flip side, better redpointers probably practice redpointing more often and have more effective scripts for memorizing beta, breaking routes down into components, and mentally dealing with failed attempts.

What Neuroscience Tells Us About Control

Okay, it is important to admit that some of our suggestions about re-scripting are easier said than done. It is good to keep expectations realistic, so that we don't beat ourselves up when progress slows down or give up because it's not what we expected. All these suggestions take a lot of trial and error, practice, drills. We will address more concrete ways to practice, but first, the neuroscience. In the buzz words of psychology, we are talking about "self-regulation"—the ability to control our own thoughts, emotions, and behaviors. In the case of fear, self-regulation is focused on "emotion-regulation," achieved in part through altering scripted habits of thinking.

Evolution has produced an amazing array of mental adaptations. The Pre-Frontal Cortex (PFC; top, front of your brain, pre-meaning a bit back from the forehead) is the brain region that produces higher-level self-regulation functions. These functions include considering the consequences of our actions and long-term planning. So, when you want to body slam your boss, but the thought of losing your job and living in poverty stops you, it is the PFC that has kicked in. The amygdala is one of the emotion centers in your brain, especially for fear. When you want to run from that interview, it's your amygdala that is influencing your thoughts and fear. So the PFC and amygdala may be in conflict in situations such as anger at your boss or fear over an interview.

Recent research has shown that the neural projections between the PFC and amygdala go both ways. The implications are: 1) fear influences your thinking; and 2) thinking can influence your emotions.

Point #2 is good news for climbers. We would like to capitalize upon this ability to control our emotions by changing our thoughts. The PFC-to-amygdala projections support Ellis's ABC model in that thinking can change feeling. However, some of that same neuroscience research suggests that there are more connections from the amygdala to the PFC than vice versa. The implication is that our control is limited. Regardless of the exact proportion in either direction, our control is restricted, not absolute. Although Ellis seems to suggest that with the proper beliefs, one never needs to experience fear or anger, the neuroscience does not back this assertion. We accept the neuroscience and believe that the idea of complete control is bull$*%^, another scientific term.

Think of an analogous situation, yogis controlling their heart rate. They are using consciousness (and the PFC) to control an automatic, autonomic bodily function. They may gain extreme control—slowing their heart rate to one beat every other day (pretty sure we're exaggerating that one), but it takes years of practice. So, while results may be rapid, they probably won't be extreme in the short-term, and they will take practice. Also, as we discussed in Chapter 2, instinctual drift and spontaneous recovery should set our expectations that in the absence of practice, our ability to control and optimize fear/arousal will slip.

Fear is Rewarding?

Let us offer a final perspective on why we should not hate our fears. Fear is part of the game; we signed up for it. Fear has been creatively framed as an "overdose of excitement," sometimes by macho-types who don't want to admit they were afraid. Sure, it occasionally reaches levels that we didn't anticipate or don't enjoy, but that ever-present threat is one of the things that makes climbing so rewarding, even addictive. The key to this addictive quality is the joy of pulling through and succeeding when your mind is screaming "stop." To quote Mark Twain, "Courage is resistance to fear, mastery of fear—not absence of fear." Conquering our fears, performing in spite of our fears, provides a sense of mastery that we may not often enjoy in our "normal" lives. Thus, overcoming fear is an example of the Mastery Motivation we discussed in Chapter 3. In this way, fear, pride, and joy are all related.

Furthermore, the arousal-fear-performance relationships run deeper than discussed in this chapter. Optimal performance, pride, and joy are parts of the "flow experience" or "being in the zone," the topic of Chapter 10. As we will see in that chapter, entering the zone is partially dependent on the level of challenge, including the challenges provided by fear.

Before we discuss flow, we will apply the science of fear to two specific fears present in climbing. Fear of Falling is the topic of Chapters 5 and 6. Fear of Failure is the topic of Chapters 7 and 8. A better understanding of these common fears and how to control them will provide you with tools needed to achieve flow.

5

The Fear of Falling

By Don McGrath

> Gravity is a contributing factor in nearly 73 percent of accidents involving falling objects.
>
> – Dave Barry

The fear of falling is a basic human instinct. The loss of control and the potential for bodily harm make this a powerful fear that holds many climbers back. I am very aware of the impact that the fear of falling has on me when I'm climbing. When I climb above my last piece of protection, the fear of falling kicks in. It may stay with me until I clip the next piece of protection. Have you ever clipped a bolt from a hard or awkward position, only to find a great stance after making the clip? Nearly all climbers who lead climb have experienced this at least once. It is a powerful example of how the fear of falling affects our thinking and our judgment while climbing.

Why do we fear falling? We may fear it because there is a risk of injuring ourselves, a very rational fear. We may also fear falling because we do not want to have to reclimb a section of a route. This type of fear is an expression of our ego. We don't want to face the fact that we have to repeat that section because we failed to make it to the next protection point. We may even become angry. However, if you are lead climbing, you must get to the next protection point to avoid having to repeat sections of the route. As such, this type of fear of falling is not rational, as it denies the nature of lead climbing.

The Need for Falling

Whether you like to admit it or not, if you want to climb at a level above 5.10 or 5.11, you will fall. In fact, you should fall—a lot. Certainly, most climbers progress more quickly if they push their limits to falling. At advanced or elite levels, falling is part of climbing. If you want to climb at this level, you must learn to manage your fear of falling. In order to improve performance, you must replace old fear-based scripts with more effective scripts. As a bonus, climbing will become more fun. Terror has a funny way of taking the fun out of climbing.

In order to manage your fear of falling you must be able to quickly assess the true risk of a potential fall when faced with a decision to proceed or not. Developing this ability is not an easy or fast process, but in the upcoming section we will explain a decision-making framework that will help you. With practice, making these decisions about risk will become scripted, allowing you to make better decisions more quickly.

Fall Factors—Overview

There are four main factors to consider when deciding whether to proceed in the face of a fall. You must consider the likelihood of a fall, the chance of injury if you fall, severity of the potential injury, and your desire to do the climb. Your decision hinges on a four-dimensional tradeoff of these factors. The likelihood of a fall is the probability that you'll take the fall should you proceed. The probability ranges from nearly zero percent or very unlikely, to almost certain.

Fall Factor 1—Fall Likelihood

When I climbed in the Gunks, I would often climb 20 or 30 feet between protection points on easy sections of climbs. The likelihood of a fall in these instances was very low, and I felt that moving through them more quickly was beneficial. I would often climb past good gear placements because I was comfortable. I was confident of my judgment for many reasons. Often I had done the route before, and I knew the terrain ahead was easy. I was also very familiar with climbing this type of rock, a quartzited sandstone. I knew what 5.7 climbing felt like here, and I climbed miles of it in the Gunks. My repeated experiences allowed me to develop scripts that included confidence and calmness in spite of runouts and skipping placements. These scripts enabled better performance.

On the other hand, there are times when I know that a fall is nearly certain. When I am working on any climb in the 5.12 or 5.13 range, I am likely to fall at the crux. I often know or suspect the crux's location, and so I am prepared to make an assessment of the fall risk when I get there.

When the likelihood of taking a fall is somewhere between unlikely and almost certain, we face some of the most exhilarating moments in climbing. You may be onsighting at your limit, where there's a good chance you will fall. If you've done a significant amount of leading, you'll likely have experienced a situation where you doubted your ability to pull off a move. You may have known what to do, but were pumped and tired. Or you may have suspected you had the right beta, but were not sure you could use the holds. You may also have known what to do immediately, but were uncertain how to continue once past the move.

It is these "now or never" moments that tweak our brains and create powerful emotional experiences. When we pull through and make these moves successfully, our bodies are awash with excitement and emotion, cementing these memories like few others. These moments of success under duress are highly rewarding and are likely to become scripted. Lynn Hill unknowingly described her script formation in a Climbing Magazine interview way back in 1987. Russ Raffa shared his observation that Lynn expects to succeed 98% of the time when she faces a crux, where for most climbers it's more like 50%.

Lynn Hill: "Maybe that's learned too, because I've been rewarded by going for it so many times that it's easier for me to make the positive choice. I think you can teach yourself to fail just as you can teach yourself to succeed."

Indeed, you can teach yourself to fail or succeed. That's exactly our goal in writing this book. Identifying maladaptive scripts and understanding how to change them are the keys to mental training.

When projecting a route, you eventually reach a point where your probability of success is reasonably high. If you've projected routes, then you know when you reach this point. It is at this time when you wait for the best conditions, maybe until the climb is in the shade. You leave all unnecessary gear on the ground, even leaving behind your hold brush to lighten your weight. You may use your lightest "send rope" or wear your lucky neon lycra tights (a superstitious script!). You launch into the route, executing your well-rehearsed sequences, conserving energy so you can make your best effort at the crux. You know what to do, but you have never done the crux from the ground before. At the rest just below the crux, you shake out your arms, take a few deep breaths and go. Left hand crosses under your right to the sharp undercling. Your right hand reaches up for the shallow pinch, which you latch, feeling your hand find the optimal placement and the thumb catch. You lift your right foot to the waist-high flake out right, subtly twisting your left hip into the wall. You quickly thrutch your left hand to the flat undercling side-pull, making sure to find the subtle thumb catch there too. Moving quickly now, you move your right foot to the good hold under you, followed by the high left step to the pencil eraser-like nubbin. Your right foot shoots out to the small black edge. With your hands starting to lose power on the poor holds, you thrust your hips into the wall and throw your right hand to the slopey side-pull. You did it! You were anxious, but not too fearful. In fact, my hands are sweating just writing about these moves on my latest project, *Sexy Beast* in Rifle Mountain Park.

Likelihood is an important consideration when evaluating the true risk of taking a climbing fall. However, it interacts with the other important factors.

Fall Factor 2—Likelihood of Injury

The second important factor to consider is the likelihood of an injury to you or your partner. If a fall is highly unlikely, then you can tolerate high consequences. If a fall is highly likely, you need to ensure that the fall is unlikely to result in any injury for you or your belayer. If the fall likelihood is in between, you also need to ensure that the fall is safe for you and your belayer. This aspect of your decision-making framework is nonlinear, in that if the fall likelihood is 50%, you would not proceed if the chance of getting an injury were 50%. Most climbers will only proceed when the risk of injury from a fall is insignificant or if they are fairly certain that they will not fall.

Countless factors affect the risk of injury from a fall. Six of the most important are listed below, arranged to form the acronym LESSON.

- LESS than vertical terrain: If the terrain is less than vertical, is there any chance that you will fall backward, upside down? Our legs are very good at absorbing forces from a fall as we come to rest against the wall, while our head and shoulders are terrible at this. You also have far more to lose by breaking a head in contrast to a leg. It is for these reasons that falls on less than vertical terrain can be the most dangerous.

- EXPERIENCED belayer: Is your belayer used to catching you on similar falls? The belayer's response to a fall is just as important as what the climber does. The belayer needs to be able to read the fall danger and provide the right response to make the fall safe and pleasant for the climber.

Just as you practice falling, you should have your belayer practice catching you in various fall scenarios.

- SWING potential: If you are climbing more than a foot or two left or right of your protection, will you swing into a wall or protrusion?

- SIMILAR falls: Is the fall significantly longer than you're used to? Proper falling requires practice. And longer falls require different skills. You should slowly build your experience base of falling. We will discuss this at length later.

- OBJECTS to hit: Will the fall result in you hitting a ledge or protrusion? People don't get hurt falling; it's the sudden deceleration that causes injury. Your fall zone should be clear of such ledges and protrusions.

- NEED to clear a roof: If you're climbing above the lip of a roof, is there a chance that you will swing into the lip and hit your knees, shoulders or head? If so, your belayer needs to give you enough slack to put you below the lip of the roof.

Below is the LESSON Checklist that you can use to evaluate a potential fall:

- LESS - is the rock less than vertical?
- EXPERIENCED - is my belayer experienced catching this type of potential fall?
- SWING - is there a chance I will swing into something?
- SIMILAR - have I experienced similar falls?
- OBJECTS - are there objects to hit?
- NEED - do I need to clear the lip of a roof?
- The LESSON Checklist captures the most common injury-causing fall scenarios.

Fall Factor 3—Severity of the Injury

In addition to the likelihood of falling and getting injured, you need to consider the severity of the injury. Figure 5.1 illustrates a decision-making framework that incorporates the likelihood and severity of injury in a fall. The figure shows how I would decide whether to proceed on a route or not. The line indicates the boundary which separates when I would or would not go for it. Below the line I would go for it, while above the line I would not. Along the bottom, representing cases where a fall would only result in a bump or a bruise, I would most likely go for it. I would only hesitate toward the bottom-right where the lump or bruise would be certain. In that case, I might hang and rest or consider options to optimize my chance of success and avoid the bump or bruise.

In cases where the fall could result in a debilitating injury, such as an ankle sprain or broken bone, the only way that I would proceed is if I judged that the injury is highly unlikely. These cases are represented by the zone halfway up the graph. An example of this is a route where I have the potential to hit the lip of a roof. If I were confident in my belayer's abilities and they had caught me safely in similar situations, I might proceed. I have often been faced with a situation where I felt that a fall would likely result in an ankle sprain, so I decided not to do the climb.

I made this decision recently on a climb named *ODK*, a 5.12a in the Poudre River Canyon in Colorado. The crux is at the second bolt and lies just above a blocky slab. I was initially hesitant to lead the climb because of the likelihood of hurting my ankle, which I had sprained badly a few times in the past. My climbing

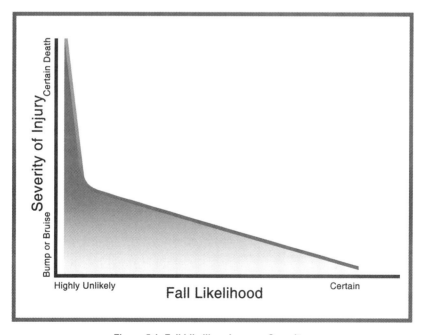

Figure 5.1: Fall Likelihood versus Severity.

partner John had been on the route before and he said that he was initially worried about the fall too, but that he had safely taken the fall. I happily let him lead the climb, although I hoped he didn't fall at the crux. John climbed easily up to the crux at the second bolt, clipping both bolts en route.

After a brief pause, he launched into a powerful layback crux. He put his right foot on the small smear and moved his left hand to a gaston. Reaching his right hand up to the small edge, he popped off the rock. The rope went taut as I caught him. I was surprised to see that he didn't even come close to hitting the slab because the route was so steep. Seeing is believing. Having seen the fall was safe, and trusting John's belay ability, I decided to lead the route that day. It's a great route and I'm happy I did it.

The moral of this story is that it's sometimes a good idea to watch someone else take a fall if it concerns you. It's often hard to imagine a fall accurately, and seeing the fall firsthand can alleviate your fears or confirm them. Watching someone else take a safe fall is the next best thing to experiencing the fall yourself, when it comes to learning about the fall consequence.

Returning to Figure 5.1, when the severity of an injury is certain death (along the top of the graph), the only time I will proceed is when the likelihood of a fall is highly unlikely— the far left. Many people would not even proceed then, but this is my personal comfort level. The best example that I can give comes from a recent trip to Cayman Brac, a small island in the Caribbean. "The Brac" has about 50 very good sport climbs. One of the premiere walls, The Point, is situated on a bluff, rising out of the sea. To get to the base of the routes, climbers must locate anchors over the lip of the bluff and rappel down to anchors at the start of the routes.

If you are experienced with rope work and rappelling, the likelihood of falling from the top of the cliff is very, very low. The consequence, however, of falling into the deep, crashing sea below is certain death. Some experienced ocean swimmers might survive such a plummet, but I would certainly not. When I first did this rappel, I was definitely nervous, but confident in the safety system that I was using. I was able to carry out the rappel and lead routes at the bluff only because I felt that the chance of taking the plunge to certain death was extremely low.

I know many people who would not get within 20 feet of the edge of that cliff, and this depends on your personal comfort level. It is my experience that the variation in comfort levels around potentially dangerous situations is a function of how many times you have been in similar situations. I recall being scared as a new climber, while being lowered on a top-rope only 30 feet off the ground. I now can stand on a ledge hundreds of feet off the ground as long as I'm anchored in. I have habituated to the exposure and now my scripts involving heights generally arouse low levels of fear. People who see pictures of me in high places tell me that they could never do that because they are afraid of heights. They have very different scripts. I usually ask them if they have ever skied or ridden a bicycle. If they have, I suggest that getting used to heights is similar to getting used to going faster on skis or on a bicycle. When you do these activities often, you get comfortable going faster and faster, until you can go at speeds that would have scared you silly when you started.

Fall Factor 4—Desire

The final factor in the decision-making framework for falling is how much you desire to do the specific climb. Most of us are inspired by certain climbs because of how they look, their location or their historical significance. And if we're very inspired to do a particular climb, we may be more willing to risk a fall.

I have, for example, done a few climbs with an "R" protection rating because of their allure. In general, I stick to the climbs that have a gear rating of "G" or "PG." I know several people who have done the *Bachar-Yerian* in Tuolumne Meadows, with its legendary 40-foot runouts on 5.11+ knob climbing, because of the route's mystique. I also know of cases where climbers backed off climbs that were not particularly hard or dangerous because the climb failed to inspire them. The relationship between desire and risk tolerance is illustrated in Figure 5.2. The shaded area below the line represents cases where I would go for it, while the region above the line shows cases where I would not.

Most of us avoid taking significant risks on climbs that we're not super excited about. And, even then, most of us have only moderate tolerance for significant risk. So, our decision-making framework has four dimensions, which makes it very difficult to illustrate on paper. To do this, I break the model up into two three-dimensional images as shown in Figures 5.3 and 5.4.

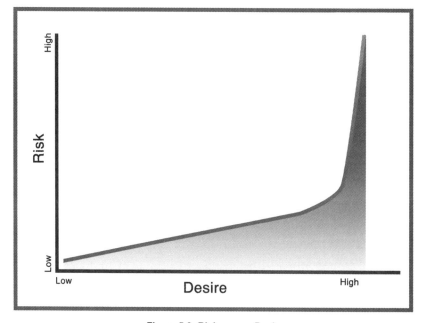

Figure 5.2: Risk versus Desire.

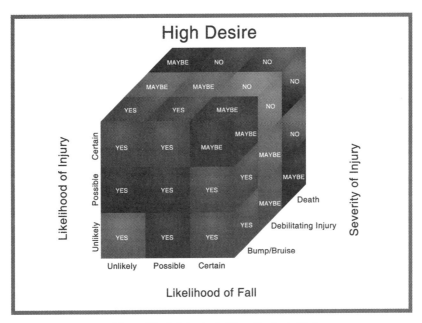

Figure 5.3: Fall Analysis When Desire is High.

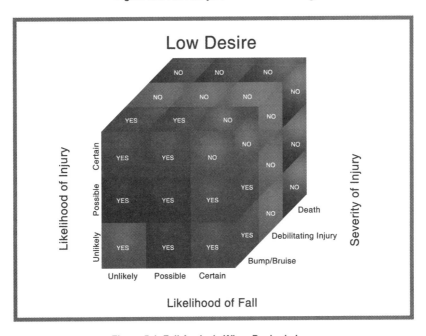

Figure 5.4: Fall Analysis When Desire is Low.

Notice in Figure 5.3, that when a fall is unlikely and injury from a fall is unlikely, I will go for it. My decision is indicated by a "yes" in the boxes representing those regions. As the likelihood of the fall increases and the likelihood of even a minor injury goes up, I hesitate to commit, indicated by the "maybe" in the box.

At the back side of the cube in Figure 5.3, where Death is the severity of the injury, I am unlikely to go for it unless the probability of falling is very low. While you cannot see the entire backside of the cube, it would be filled with "no" and "maybe," without a single "yes."

The only difference between Figures 5.3 and 5.4 is that many of the maybe blocks turn to "no." I'm less inclined to take risk on climbs that I'm not that excited about.

Create Your Fear of Falling Profile

Use the following slices of this model to discover your own decision-making profile when evaluating fall consequences. In each box, write your evaluation (no, maybe, or yes) based on the four variables: desire, severity of injury, likelihood of fall, likelihood of injury.

Now you have the fall decision-making framework to profile how to proceed on a climb where you face a potential fall. You probably looked at your profile and wondered how you will use this information when you're climbing. It's not practical for you to memorize these profiles, so what good are they? The utility of the profiles comes not from using it in the moment of truth on your next route, but in other situations. First, you can use it to size up decisions on routes where you can see the dangers from the ground or from an adjacent climb. Second, you can use it to make decisions about a project that you have backed off of, top-roped, or climbed safely via stick-clipping. Third, you can use it to come to grips with your personal level of tolerance to risk of injury. Although nothing is static, the profile that you mapped out will look similar if you were to take it again one year from now or five years from now. Fourth, with repeated application, you will be able to implement decision-making quickly, so that you can use it in the moment.

High Desire
Severity of Injury-Death

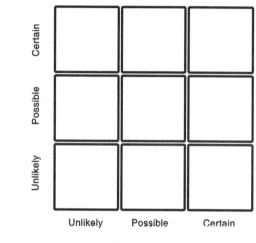

Likelihood of Fall

High Desire
Severity of Injury-Bump/Bruise

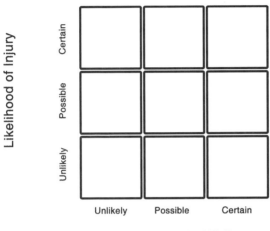

High Desire
Severity of Injury-Debilitating Injury

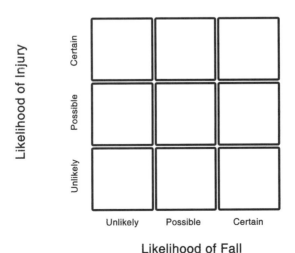

SUPER Climbing

The following is an expanded process that you can run through to aid in decision-making in the moment, when you are faced with fall potential. We call it the SUPER method. You will need 30 seconds or so to run through this process, so it is not that useful in desperate situations, but the more you use it, the faster you will be able to execute it. In other words, this process is a script and, with practice, it will become faster and easier to implement in the heat of the moment. It will eventually be useful in desperate situations when you only have seconds to make a decision.

When faced with the decision of how to proceed, do the following:

- Shift Focus: The first step is to shift your focus. Open your focus from a narrow, execution-based focus to an open focus where you take in all of your surroundings, notice every potential hold and determine your objective. Take the time to find the stance you're aiming for, which likely is where you'll clip the next bolt or place the next piece of gear. Examine potential paths and holds, looking to the left and the right, as well as directly up. Notice features, chalk marks, and boot-rubber marks. Take in your entire surroundings. As with all these steps, it will take time and repetition before you reliably execute this script to consistently focus your attention.

- Understand: This is to understand the fall and the fall consequences. Are there objects to hit? Is there a lip of a roof to hit? Are there objects to swing into? Where will the gear be as you get to the next stance? How good is your gear? Are you comfortable with the gear and the fall? If not, improve the gear if possible.

- Plan: Plan your strategy. If you're comfortable with the fall, then decide on the strategy you'll take to get to the next stance.

- Execute: The next step is to execute the plan. Shift to narrow, execution-based focus. If you encounter something unexpected down low, retreat and rethink your strategy. If you hit the unexpected up high, remain relaxed, open your focus, determine your best option and execute.

- Relax: Relax at the stance and place protection. Relaxation is a very general purpose script that applies to everyday situations, but it's one of the most important in climbing. We will address tips on relaxation later.

The first three steps are thinking steps. In the first two, you take in your surroundings and situation to understand your options and fall consequences. The third step—plan—is where you decide on a course of action. The fourth step—execute—is when you shift from thinking to acting. It is important for this shift to be abrupt and conscious. In order to make this shift abrupt, I suggest you take a few quick breaths signaling the shift. At first, doing this consciously will feel strange, but over time your brain will come to recognize this signal as the trigger to initiate your script that takes you from thinking to acting.

Carrying out the fourth step may result in a shift back to thinking if the unexpected is encountered. The unexpected takes us out of autopilot mode. When this happens, go to Step 1, then 3 and 4, skipping Step 2. You've already decided your gear is good, so there's no need to do this again. At first, it may be natural for you to reexamine your gear, but try and focus on climbing and not the fall consequences, unless you now see a new risk element. The goal should be to analyze the fall when you are calmly at the initial stance.

You now have a framework to help you understand your tolerance for risk of injury in a fall, as well as some suggestions on how to improve your mindset for more successful and safe climbing. In addition, you have a process you can use when making a decision on whether to proceed and how to proceed on a climb. Using this process will help you have the right focus at the right time, leading to more successful and safe climbing.

In the next chapter, we present drills that you can do to help you create more productive scripts and help you manage your fear of falling. Practicing these drills will dramatically improve your climbing and increase your enjoyment by easing your fear of falling, enabling you to better focus on the task at hand—climbing.

6 Falling and Relaxation Drills and Tactics

By Jeff Elison

❝ Practice does not make perfect. Only perfect practice makes perfect.

– Vince Lombardi

The focus of the previous Fear of Falling chapter was on a framework for risk analysis and a process for analyzing falls. However, there are other very concrete steps we can take to address the fear of falling. Our discussion will move from what you can do to size-up and become more comfortable with specific falls to how you can become more comfortable with falling, in general. Then we address relaxation and recovery. Finally, we will address common maladaptive scripts many of us deploy when confronted with a hard move, like freezing.

How to Use This Chapter

This chapter encompasses three types of tips. The first type consists of mental strategies for assessing specific falls. You can add these to your mental toolkit and pull them out as needed. The second type consists of drills to help you get more comfortable with falling. These are things you can actually do, actions you can practice, to reduce fear. The third type consists of suggestions for re-scripting. That means you have to identify problematic scripts, replace them with something more constructive, and mentally practice them. To help you, we describe some common scripts many of us deploy when confronted with a hard move, like freezing and procrastinating. And we offer alternatives to replace them.

Specific Falls

Let's start by considering specific falls. For example, revisit the Poudre Canyon example where Don was concerned about the potential for hitting a ledge, were he to fall between the second and third bolts. In that example, he was reassured by watching a partner take the fall safely. In many cases like this, we can watch other people take the fall that has us worried.

Seb Grieve took another innovative approach on the nightmare route Parthian Shot in the Peak District of the U.K. Parthian Shot is an extremely hard gritstone trad route with big fall potential onto a questionable flake. Seb placed the gear, threaded the rope through it, hiked around to the top and threw sandbags off the top to test the flake. It held and he ended up taking that fall multiple times on redpoint attempts before making the second ascent. Some of this action is documented in the video *Hard Grit*. Just like Don watching his partner, others were reassured. Parthian Shot saw at least six repeats before Will Stanhope took the fall, broke the flake, ripped the gear, and took a 40' bone-crushing ground fall. Is there a lesson here? Maybe two: Be innovative and there are no guarantees in climbing!

When you can't toss sandbags and don't have a sucker (I mean partner) who is willing to take the fall in order to show you it is safe, you can work up to it yourself. For example, a leader might opt to clip the second bolt and let go. If safe, they might then climb two feet above the bolt and jump off, and then four feet... You will get a better idea of the fall path and how close you will come to any obstacles. Eventually you can climb to the next bolt (or piece) or find that you can safely take the maximal fall—should you fail right at the next bolt.

Similarly, fear of a specific fall may be messing with your head and your performance on a redpoint. To overcome this situation, don't just practice the moves, practice the fall. In fact, fear of the fall may be interfering with your ability to practice the beta. Go up a few feet and jump off. Continue until you are comfortable with falling from the moves that concern you. Psychologists call this *habituation*—getting used to a situation to the point where you don't notice it anymore or your reaction is reduced. The mental mechanism of habituation is what happens when you walk into a room with a bad odor, and after a few minutes you stop noticing it.

On a recent project, I had to commit to a dyno to a 2-finger pocket 70' up a route. Every failed attempt resulted in a 20' fall. My first few "attempts" weren't real attempts; each consisted of climbing a bit higher and tossing with more commitment. These attempts were more about testing the worst-case fall than wiring the beta. Worst case, my fingers would barely catch the pocket and I'd take the biggest possible whipper. I did this several times "off-the-dog" (after hanging) and learned not to fear it. That allowed me to commit 100% during redpoint attempts.

Falling is Fun

"I'm going to go ahead boldly because a little bird told me
That jumping is easy, that falling is fun . . .
Up until you hit the sidewalk, shivering, and stunned."
– Ani DiFranco, Swan Dive

Moving another step toward the general, you can easily practice safe falls at the gym or on routes. If you fear falling, even safe falls, then I guarantee that this is a script that is holding you back. Rush right to your gym with a belayer you trust, pick a nice easy overhanging route with no obstacles to hit, climb up and let go. If this scares you, then start now. I mean it! You can start by taking falls on top-rope. Ask your belayer to give you 6 inches of slack, then a foot, then 2 feet, etc. Before you know it, you will be comfortable taking 10-footers. In the process, you will also learn something about how to fall. At first, many people instinctively do several things: grab the rope, tense up, and hold their breath. Watch beginner climbers take a few falls and these mistakes will be visible. The climber hits the end of the rope, his stiff legs bang the wall with a thud, and you can hear the air being released from his lungs, "umph." Instead, stay relaxed, stay vertical, don't grab the rope. Bring your feet up in front of you as you come into the wall to let your legs absorb the shock. These lessons are better learned during a planned, controlled fall rather than during an unanticipated fall on questionable terrain. Thus, practice falls will actually increase your safety.

On lead, make sure your belayer is prepared and then let go when a bolt is at your waist. Then 6 inches below your waist, a foot, etc. This is an incredibly easy way to habituate and rewrite that pesky script that is holding you back. In fact, why are you still reading this when you could be in your car on the way to the gym by now?

The Falling Habit

To address fear of falling at the most general level, make falls a habit. Keep that new script tuned up. Remember the principles of spontaneous recovery and instinctual drift. They tell us that fear of falling will probably return if we don't fall for a while. If you can't climb for a period of time, then make practice falls part of your routine when you return to climbing.

But wait, there's more…order before midnight and… just kidding. Recalling the mechanics of fear, there is more to be gained by addressing your fear of falling. Reducing your fear of falling will lead to gains in thinking, focus, attention, and memory. During precision moves, your focus needs to be precise. On the project I just described, I found it hard to concentrate on that pocket as I prepared to dyno. It seemed like my peripheral vision was blurring my focus. In reality, it was my fear pulling my attention to what came next—the fall and my trajectory. Once I practiced the fall and put fear out of my mind, I could get down to business. I'd assume the position I had wired, sag down, and suddenly nothing else existed but that pocket. It was like a baseball player keeping his eye on the ball until the moment of contact, something I could not do when afraid.

Relaxation, Breathing, and Focus

When we described scripting and how to change scripts, we suggested that one good time to practice is on your warm-up climbs. I'd like to take that a step further. Most of us embrace the physical benefits of warming up, such as injury prevention and avoiding the "flash pump." However, warm ups are a great time to work on your mental game. Not only is it a time to pursue the Path Effect (laying down new scripts), it is a time to warm up mentally. By mentally, I mean your focus, attention, relaxation, and confidence. Don't waste your warm-up time. If you are climbing at your local crag, you may have climbed every warm up dozens of times. Instead of just going through the motions, you can concentrate your attention and hone your focus in anticipation of the challenges you will face later in the day.

Breathing is another key to relaxation, fear control, and improved performance. The fight-or-flight response often causes us to breathe more rapidly, shallowly, with tension in our chests. Yoga practitioners are intimately familiar with the benefits of proper breathing. So are many climbers. "If I can just breathe well" was one of several factors that Marc Le Menestrel mentioned in his quest to make the third ascent of Just Do It—America's first 5.14c, at Smith Rock.

Breathing seems pretty automatic and simple, so what does it mean to breathe well? It depends. In the previous chapter, we suggested taking a few quick breaths to shift from planning to action, as a trigger to initiate your scripted plan. That is ideal when you need to get amped to tackle that redpoint crux. However, recalling the Performance-Arousal Curve, we may want to increase or decrease arousal to obtain the optimal level and highest performance. Scripts are triggered by specific stimuli, and breathing correlates so well with your level of arousal that breathing rituals are ideal for initiating scripts—amping up or calming down as the situation demands. Like the weightlifter fondling the bar before a maximal bench press, a few rapid forceful breaths oxygenate your blood and increase your arousal. But if you are on the other side of the curve and need to bring your arousal down for the next section of your onsight or that delicate slab move, then a few slow, deep breaths may be more effective. In fact, with practice these slow breaths can trigger what Benson called the Relaxation Response in his book by that title in 1975.

The bottom line is that you want to develop and practice two different sets of scripts (i.e., amp up or calm down) to achieve optimal arousal. Breathing can be the trigger to initiate both. Understanding the Performance-Arousal Curve, how it works for you, and training yourself to control your levels of arousal will enable you to achieve optimal performance. Lack of such insight may hinder your performance. I have a partner who routinely takes three deep breaths before leaving the ground. Unfortunately, I can hear the stress in those breaths. They broadcast worry and over-arousal. So, I doubt they are helping him to achieve his goal, to reduce anxiety. Similarly, I'll never forget climbing with two guys at Wild Iris in the early '90s. While the better climber was attempting to send, his partner would literally scream BREATHHHHHHHHE! I nearly wet myself with fear and I wasn't even climbing!

The latter example suggests another tactic. When your attention and working memory are overloaded with the demands of the moment, partners can help. A properly presented suggestion to relax or to breathe well (said in a calm voice, just loud enough to hear) can be a huge aid. In chapter 9, you will learn more about how to effectively coach other climbers like this.

Finally, there are entire books on relaxation techniques, such as the old classic *The Relaxation Response* by Benson. It is useful to think about what you are doing in terms of his title. You are exerting mental self-control to reduce mental arousal, which will in turn reduce physiological arousal, and hopefully move you to where you need to be on the Performance-Arousal Curve. That's a lot of words to say: You are calming down mentally to calm down physically. But Benson's title suggests an important dynamic: stimulus →RESPONSE. That coveted relaxation response is a response to well-practiced triggers. Breathing is one. Closing your eyes could be another. Visualizing your "Happy Place" like Happy Gilmore could be another (seriously). Mantras are also effective.

But you need to shop around, try them, practice them to find what works for you. Once again, practice is required to change neural connections, create scripts, and become effective. Effective means your script creates the response you desire. Unless I'm bouldering or working a route that has a power crux right off the ground, I feel like I need to reduce arousal. Before leaving the ground, my practiced triggers are three slow, deep breaths, followed by a shrug of the shoulders and saying aloud "It's just rock climbing." Sometimes I'll add, "I'll either fall or I won't." My implicit message to myself is that I'll be fine either way. Neither result will make or break my future. These messages help to reduce feelings of pressure and fear, thus reducing arousal.

What is this coveted Relaxation Response? Obviously, reduced fear and anxiety, and better breathing. However, it should also include reduced muscle tension, better concentration and better focus. Being able to trigger your own relaxation response soon after getting to a rest will allow you to maximize the benefits of resting. If you find yourself leaving a good rest still pumped, tense, and breathing too rapidly, then you haven't trained your-self sufficiently. The good news is that you have identified a weakness and you know what to work on—you have an opportunity to improve.

It is also valuable to be able to initiate something like the Relaxation Response under duress—when you are stressed. Let's call it a Reset to trigger the relaxation response script. We have already mentioned the common experience of struggling to clip a bolt or place a piece of pro and then suddenly being able to relax on those same holds once you are clipped. That makes sense; it is rational because now you are safe. However, that fear and tension are decreasing your safety before you clip. Why not reset and relax to increase your chances of making the clip or placing the piece? This is a clear example of scripting. Find a trigger—that's how I visualize my reset—and practice it.

For the last few years, I've also embraced what I call a *Time Out* when I have limited time to prevent a fall. Unlike a full Re-set → Relaxation Response script, which can be used at clipping stances and longer rests, my script for a time out lasts mere seconds. I deploy it when I need to defuse my panic script. I started by employing the Time Out when I had judged the situation to be safe, yet I knew I was wasting energy due to stress—typically over my performance. As an example, when I recently chose the wrong sequence that took me away from the much better holds, I felt the panic rise. I was pretty sure I was going to fall. I quickly assessed the fall potential and knew injury wasn't a concern. This was all about performance. I was on bad holds, but not that bad. At my current level of arousal (worry), I thought I had about five seconds left in my forearms. I accepted that my chances of pulling this off were best served by relaxing and then working it out, rather than continuing to thrash my free hand all about. I initi-ated a Time Out: I closed my eyes, took a couple of deep breaths, and relaxed. This allowed me to stop overgripping, refocus my attention, and think more clearly. I was actually surprised when I found a way out.

Many studies demonstrate that the way we label and think about situations affects their effectiveness. We can easily lead ourselves to some outcome (good or bad) just by believing or expecting it, a self-fulfilling prophecy. The more clearly we can visualize the outcome or the needed steps, the better. So, make your mental scripts concrete, something you can picture. Actions are easier to visualize than thoughts. For example, you can picture clipping the chains better than you can picture the thought of success. So, telling ourselves we have effective tools or a routine reassures us and works better than just saying: "Don't freak out." That's why I like the labels reset, time out, and relaxation response because they seem like actions I can visualize and control.

I like "Relaxation RESPONSE" as a term because it emphasizes the outcome—relaxing. The Reset is part of the Relaxation Response script. It is the antecedent or trigger that gets it started. I like "Reset" because it gives me a very tangible visual image. I just push that mental button and I'm on my way to relaxing and recovering. "Reset" also emphasizes the trigger and suggests I have control—I can trigger the desired response at will. Similarly, "Time Out" provides me with a concrete image of putting the situation on hold for a few seconds, just like pushing a pause button. The labels "Time Out" and "Reset" remind me I have more tools in my repertoire to deal with those moments when panic is knocking at my door.

The Brook Trout and Other Relaxation Tricks

I remember reading an article on running form many years ago, while I was in my brief triathlon phase. The article focused on relaxation, specifically, relaxing any muscle that wasn't propelling you forward or maintaining your posture. Clenched hands, tight jaw? They just waste valuable energy. The author illustrated the point with a cartoon drawing of a runner, lower-half human, upper-half brook trout, with its mouth loosely hanging open. I love the way the brook trout image conveys relaxation. Of course, all of this applies to climbing, especially while you are at rests or moving on easier terrain. Relax unnecessary muscle tension for maximum recovery and to save energy.

Even when you are moving, you can relax the muscles that aren't propelling you or maintaining contact. As you move a hand between holds, there is no need to keep it tense. Grab a mini-shake for a second. When I described the swimming drills in Chapter 2, I left out one of the coach's goals. As I moved my arm through the air, with my elbow up and hand down, he wanted me to relax my hand and wrist. Do the same while you are climbing. In fact, you can turn this into a drill to lay down a scripted habit of relaxation. Practice on a warm up by briefly shaking and relaxing each hand between every handhold. You may look a bit spastic if you exaggerate this drill like I did in swimming, but it will be more effective at establishing your new script.

If you find yourself too tense at good rests, unable to achieve the relaxation response discussed previously, the problem is mental. Perhaps you are too focused on the outcome, raising your anxiety. Or perhaps you are focused inward, overly aware of your physical state. Looking outward can be helpful in these cases. Take in the view. Hopefully, you are climbing in this area because it is appealing. Take a second to appreciate its beauty, instead of focusing inward. This past year, I put this to use several times on a 5.12c at Rifle, *Extended Family*. It's a very long, over-hanging climb with a major rest at about 70', just before a 3-bolt crux. I had to de-pump as much as possible in order to finish. Part of my routine at the rest was to look down-canyon and re-mind myself why I loved Rifle. Relaxation and stress reduction are proven benefits of happiness!

Freezing

Three more maladaptive scripts motivated by fear of falling and fear of failure are freezing, procrastination, and what I call half-stepping. Recall that the first step in changing scripts is to raise problems to awareness. So, if these scripts sound familiar, then you may have something to work on. Freezing is usually the result of indecision—is it better to fall from here, downclimb, or go for it? Becoming more skilled at evaluating your safety and risk of falling reduces freezing. As Lynn Hill expressed in her in-terview, you can tip the balance toward the positive, toward go-ing for it. But you can't tip the balance without actually going for it sometimes. You need to succeed in order to rewrite that script. In order to succeed, you first need to try. So, that's the drill. Prac-tice recognizing when you are freezing up and tell yourself you just need to "poop or get off the pot," as my father always said.

Freezing due to being overly cautious can be the result of nu-merous factors: history with a bad fall, being a new or inexpe-rienced climber, or an extensive background in trad climbing. Being old(er), I started climbing before sport climbing existed. When I made the transition to sport, my biggest weakness was freezing when I was on the verge of falling. It was a tradeoff be-cause it pretty much guaranteed that I would fall, but by not try-ing I wouldn't fall as far. As my biggest weakness, tackling this script held the potential for the greatest gains. Supportive partners really helped. I'm not close to perfect. I still freeze on occasion, but I've tipped the balance a long way toward going for it. A drill or tactic here is to enlist the help of partners. If you trust them, they can help you make the decision by encouraging you when it is safe.

Based on my own experience, I've been able to help other climbers. Early in his climbing career, freezing up was clearly my partner Joe's greatest weakness. He wanted to overcome it and he was open to help. He was very responsive to encouragement in the form of being yelled at. It worked. As long as the fall was safe, I'd literally yell at him: "Go for it" or "Just grab one more hold." I evaluated the situation and made the decision for him. It was as if I took the burden of decision off of his shoulders. He no longer had to decide for himself. It freed his mind and attention to deal with whatever it took to try. Not everyone responds well to such encouragement, so your mileage may vary.

Procrastination

Instead of freezing, some of us procrastinate by pretending to do something. In spite of seeing what we need to do, we fiddle about, fondling anything that might be a hold, trying every ridiculous body position, fiddling with gear—instead of getting on with the obvious. A partner recently took a short layoff due to a minor injury. He came back to Rifle a few weeks later feeling like he hadn't lost much in the way of strength. But when he tried to onsight a route at his limit, he was faced with the fact that he had lost more mentally. I had just done the route, so I knew it pretty well. I watched as he hit the second set of hard moves, not yet the crux. He looked at the next obvious hold—this was Rifle, so it was the one covered in chalk with three neon tick marks and

GPS coordinates marking its location. He briefly faked a reach toward it and then settled back into his strength-sapping "rest" and proceeded to test 23 chalk-less holds (and again I exaggerate). Mentally, he just wasn't ready to make that moderately hard move, which was well within his physical abilities. It was easier mentally to search for that hidden miracle hold no one else had found until he was too tired and could justify yelling "take." I've been there; I'm not being judgmental. Moreover, he knew it. He lowered to the ground and his first words were: "That was all mental." Indeed, that's why we wrote this book—climbing is over 90% mental.

Commitment vs. Half-Stepping

Another problematic script related to freezing and procrastination is "Half-Stepping." By this, I mean trying half-heartedly. You know what I'm talking about; you've been there. You're pumped, you know the next move, you've convinced yourself you won't stick it, so you pretend to try. You go through the motions and fall. I've done it hundreds of times myself. The opposite, trying in a committed attempt to stick it, is how you want to revise the freezing script. Lynn pegged it when she pointed out that success is the reward that allows us to rewrite this script. It still amazes me how many times "one more hold" is all it takes. You thrutch for the next hold because you don't have the strength to reach it with control, your body sags as gravity pulls you down, your fingers may even slip . . . and then it all stops and you are still on. Suddenly you can adjust your hand, move your feet, stem, or grab the next hold. That one move was the only thing between you and the onsight or the send. That's why screaming "one more hold" at Joe was so effective.

Grabbing quickdraws ("choking the cobra") is another manifestation of half-stepping. Rather than commit to making the clip or taking the fall, it is easier to grab the draw. This is a potentially dangerous practice that is often followed by a desperate attempt to clip while one's hand slowly slips down the draw. Sometimes the climber makes the clip and sometimes they take the plunge. Todd Skinner had an interesting approach to re-scripting this bad habit when I ran into him at Smith Rock in the '80s (before I had ever heard of him). He made a promise to himself that whenever he grabbed a draw, he would take the penalty fall. So, he would jump, rather than clip after grabbing it.

We have presented some counterproductive scripts that represent the most common responses to the fear of falling. We have suggested drills that you can use to rewrite those scripts. Now it's your turn. Identify the scripts that you tend to exhibit and practice the associated drills to rewrite them.

Which scripts hold you back the most? You may want to jot down a few in the space below:

_____

_____

_____

_____

In the next two chapters, we discuss the fear of failure, which also holds most climbers back. Chapter 7 focuses on the definitions, theory, and science you need to understand fear of failure and to reveal problem scripts. Chapter 8 describes a list of specific scripts, along with drills to change them.

7 Fear of Failure

By Jeff Elison and Don McGrath

> I've missed more than 9000 shots in my career. I've lost almost 300 games. 26 times I've been trusted to make the game winning shot and missed. I've failed over and over and over in my life. And that is why I succeed.
>
> – Michael Jordan

We have dealt with the fear of falling, the most prevalent fear according to climbers in Don's survey. However, something else happens when you fall—you FAIL! At least, that's one way of interpreting a fall. Don and I know from personal experience that the fear of failure is a powerful force that impacts climbing performance. Although only 4% of the climbers Don surveyed felt the fear of failure was the "biggest" thing holding them back, we think that for many it is a significant factor. In fact, this underreporting is consistent with thousands of studies from social psychologists. Underreporting, including Don's mere 4%, happens for two reasons which we discuss later in this chapter. First, you will see that fear of failure often operates at unconscious levels. Second, we often use mental avoidance tactics, rather than face these particular fears. Specifically, we fear failure because failure threatens our egos, so acknowledging fear of failure requires us to admit we feel threatened. As a result, applying some of the topics in this chapter may present a personal challenge, but we think facing the challenge of self-evaluation is well worth it. We suggest you try to keep an open mind and attempt to be brutally honest with yourself as you read this chapter.

Sensitivity to evaluation by others is part of human nature. It has been around for so many thousands of generations that it operates automatically, outside our awareness. Fear of failure may be less significant for people who have been climbing for a long time and who understand that failures can speed progress; however, for most of us, the fear of failure holds us back. It often prevents us from doing exactly the thing we need to do in order to progress—push ourselves. It may also prevent us from climbing routes that are inspiring, but at our limit. When fear of failure kicks in, we pay a price in performance and enjoyment, the two things we are trying to enhance.

Fear of failure is mostly fear of looking bad in front of other people. This fear of having others judge you poorly is most obvious with glossophobia—the fear of public speaking—often rated more acute than the fear of heights or the fear of physical pain. Just as glossophobia can render a speaker paralyzed before an audience, fear of public disgrace can leave a climber powerless.

By understanding fear of failure, you will be able to identify how it operates for you, in what ways it holds you back or diminishes your enjoyment. With this understanding, you have some hope of changing those frustrating scripts. You will likely climb harder and enjoy it more.

If you still have doubts about the importance of fear of failure, consider the following example. Imagine warming up with six of your favorite partners. You are all taking turns on moderate warm ups. It's your turn and you feel like hell. You sketch, thrutch, get ridiculously pumped, and even fall. Would that bother you? Fear of failure includes situations like this one, fear of a poor performance. More specifically, it is the fear of being judged negatively by yourself or others due to performance.

Don offered the following as just one example of how fear of failure held him back:

> "When I had been climbing for about five years and had a few 5.12 routes under my belt, I recall climbing at Lost City in the Gunks and belaying my friend Fred on *Survival of the Fittest*. Survival is a classic 5.13a top-rope problem made famous when Scott Franklin became the first American to solo 5.13 with his ropeless ascent. In those days, there was always a posse of locals hanging out at the Survival Block on the weekends. They all had the route wired and would do laps on it. I recall Fred encouraging me to try and work on the climb, yet I was so intimidated

by the posse that I didn't even try. I was afraid of looking like a total gumby in front of the stronger, more-tal-
ented group. I came to know, years later, that in general
people don't care how you climb, except that, if they can
climb better than you it can make them feel a little better
about themselves. In cases like this, the posse knew that
they had the route wired and most of them got there by
initially thrashing away like I would have. They would
have probably been psyched to see me try, even if it was
a rough go. A few years later, I worked on Survival of the
Fittest, paid my dues and sent it. I think I would have
progressed more rapidly had I been able to overcome my
fear of failure sooner."

Don's story isn't unusual. I know I have hundreds like it. In
some of those stories, the ways in which the fear of evaluation
impacted my fun and progress may be as obvious as in Don's.
In others, the effects are much more subtle. I may not even have
been aware of them. It may not have been obvious that it was fear
of failure affecting me. You probably have similar stories. Most
likely, you have more than you realize. That's because fear of evaluation often operates outside our awareness—automatically and
unconsciously. By the time you finish this chapter and the next, I
hope these maladaptive dynamics become clearer, making it easier to recognize these situations and their negative effects. Doing
so will allow you to optimize your climbing experiences.

Why Fear Failure?

To manage our fear of failure, it is helpful to understand where
it comes from, why it is important, and how it operates. Humans
are a social species, a fact that has many implications. The most
important of these is that living in groups greatly increases our

probability of survival. Imagine yourself living 70,000 years ago in a band of 50 fellow hunter-gatherers. If you did something that caused you to be cast out of the group, your death was almost guaranteed. More importantly for evolution, your chances of reproduction dropped to nearly zero and your genes would not be passed onto the next generation.

Therefore, our ancestors who preferred to live in groups, who were accepted or even admired by the group, and who had skills allowing them to fit in with groups, were much more likely to pass on their genes. Just as physical characteristics (e.g., height) are influenced by genes, so are psychological traits (e.g., anxiety, introversion vs. extroversion, finding sex pleasurable). Thus, genes that promote success in group situations became more common, part of human nature. There is no need for planning, design, or consciousness for these mechanisms to be at work. The mere probabilistic fact that some people were more likely to survive and reproduce meant their genes would become increasingly common from generation to generation.

Fear of failure is one part of a whole set of evolutionary adaptations that go along with being a social species. These adaptations include:

> *Motivations:* We are motivated to hang around other people, to be accepted, to be liked, to avoid exclusion. For example, consider your degree of motivation to avoid rejection or solitary confinement.

> *Cognitions:* We automatically monitor our social status, how others respond to us, and who treats us well or poorly.

> *Emotions:* Loneliness, feelings of rejection, embarrassment, shame, guilt, and humiliation punish us when

other people think poorly of us. Pride and joy reward us when other people think well of us. Collectively, these emotions are powerful teaching aids that motivate us to learn what is "good" and "bad" in the eyes of others. Again, imagine solitary confinement, one of the cruelest of all punishments.

The Looking Glass Self

Charles Cooley captured a basic mechanism with what he called The Looking Glass Self (looking glass meaning a mirror). He reasoned that we know from our own experiences that we form impressions of other people: cool/dorky, smart/stupid, hot/ugly, strong climber/gumby. More importantly, the vast majority of those impressions involve an evaluation: good, bad, desirable, undesirable. So, other people must be doing the same—making impressions and judgments about us.

Recognizing this, Cooley's Looking Glass mechanism consists of three parts:

1. I imagine you form an impression of me (e.g., cruises 5.13 or thrashes on 5.4).
2. I imagine your evaluation (e.g., good, bad, desirable).
3. I experience some "self-relevant" emotion (e.g., embarrassment, pride).

Sometimes we are aware, possibly painfully, of this process. That's what I tried to achieve with my falling-on-your-warm-up-in-front-of-six-partners example. You would probably start thinking about their evaluations of how bad you look as soon as you started to struggle. The Looking Glass Self is pretty obvious in this example. In other cases, we don't even notice it, but it affects us. Recognizing this, a wise sociologist named Thomas Scheff formulated the Cooley-Scheff Conjecture. The conjecture is that the Looking Glass Self operates automatically (we don't have to turn it on), constantly (even when we don't want it to operate), and often invisibly (outside of consciousness). At this point, any good, traditional, red-blooded Amerikan (I'm thinking John Wayne or Larry the Cable Guy) should object: "Not me, I don't care what anyone thinks about me; you are making too big a deal of this." However, research supports Cooley and Scheff on these points.

As an example, consider the Cocktail Party Effect. As a climber, you probably don't spend tons of time at cocktail parties, but you are familiar with this effect. Imagine being at some social gathering (no alcohol required) where the place is buzzing with many conversations. You tune out all the others and focus your attention on the conversation you are in. Now someone across the room says your name. What happens? Your focus is interrupted and you are aware that someone is talking about you. You weren't consciously processing the other words in that conversation, but YOUR NAME interrupts into consciousness. How is this possible? Automatic, constant, unconscious operation of one small part of your brain—an evolutionary adaptation.

Convinced yet about the Cooley-Scheff Conjecture? Going back to that "Amerikan" comment, the United States, Australia, and the United Kingdom are the three highest scoring countries on Individualism (as opposed to Collectivism). That means we prioritize individual achievements ("Hey, look at what I did"), individual rights ("I got my gun and my gas-guzzling SUV"), and delude ourselves about the degree to which we are influenced by other people. The latter includes things like conformity ("I ain't no conformist"), persuasion ("Advertising doesn't affect me") and peer-pressure ("I don't care what other people think"). So, we all walk around thinking we are John Wayne (if you are old and male like me) or Lisbeth Salander (Dragon Tattoo girl, if you are young and female). Those of us from the U.S., Australia, and the U.K. are the least likely to accept the conjecture. But again, research shows we would be wrong to deny it.

The Sociometer—Our Social Gas Gauge

Building on the work of Cooley and Scheff, Mark Leary developed the Sociometer Model. We don't have to be the best at everything (impossible) or loved by everyone (also impossible); we just need to be accepted, admired, or loved by enough people. So, the sociometer likens these adaptations (social monitoring, embarrassment, pride, self-esteem) to a gas gauge. If we are doing well in terms of our social acceptance, then we feel positive emotions and higher self-esteem. In his analogy, the gas tank is fairly full and we don't need to make extra efforts to win people over. If most people are indifferent to us or think we suck, then we feel negative emotions and lower self-esteem. Those negative emotions are a warning—like your "low gas light"—telling us that our tank is empty, and their pain motivates us to do something about it. So, we apologize, or make excuses for poor performance, or go out of our way to impress other people, or find new friends.

A set of really impressive studies demonstrated why we perceive social exclusion as painful—because it is! Subjects were from two groups: sufferers of chronic abdominal pain or normal subjects. They were placed in a functional MRI chamber to have their brains scanned. Researchers pressed on the abdomens of those with chronic pain to cause them immediate pain. The normal subjects played a silly game of computer ball toss, but after a few minutes the ball was no longer thrown to their character. Instead, they watched helplessly as the ball was thrown between the other two characters (which they had been misleadingly told were controlled by other subjects). They felt excluded. The brain scans of the two groups demonstrated that the "emotional pain" region of the brain is piggybacked on top of the physical pain mechanism. When we experience negative emotions due to exclusion or being judged poorly, the emotional pain region triggers the physical pain region and we experience "real pain." Thus, we have metaphors like a broken heart. This is exactly the type of adaptation we would expect from evolution—a newer function (emotional pain) leveraging an older function (physical pain).

Once again, the bottom line is that the pieces of the Looking Glass Self mechanism are all "normal." Human nature is the sum total of many, many adaptations, and these mechanisms are part of human nature. All of us are social to some degree. None of us would be happy if every friend, acquaintance, and stranger acted like we didn't exist. We all experience the self-relevant emotions Cooley wrote about, finding some of them painful (e.g., embarrassment) and some pleasurable (e.g., pride).

Good, Bad, Identity, and Ego

To complicate things—and bring this back to climbing—people don't all value the same things. I had the hardest time understanding why my mother wasn't proud of my decision to suspend my college career for a while so I could climb harder! When I mentioned "good" and "bad" previously, I didn't mean in some absolute, universal sense. Even some "moral" rights and wrongs are subjective. Some people might think eating meat and wearing a bikini are bad, even moral issues, yet I feel no shame or guilt about either. (OK, so I don't look that great in a bikini…)

Sometimes we learn what other people value, especially people who we care about, and come to value the same things ourselves (e.g., the new significant other and scrapbooking). Other times, we are biased to value the things we are good at. A minority of us tried climbing and said: "Wow, I really suck at this; it's now my life's passion." Once we value something, we tend to overestimate how much other people (my mother) value it. As another example, us old trads have all heard the tales of the hordes of groupies at the top of El Cap just waiting to throw themselves at the successful big wall climbers. At least, that's how my partner convinced me to leave El Cap Meadow.

So, as climbers, we are biased to value climbing—and to think that other people do as well. In everyday terms and psychological terms, we *identify* with climbing, which is to say it becomes who we are. Or, if we haven't lost all perspective, just a part of who we are. As a recent *Climbing Magazine* editorial discussed, saying "it's just climbing" is a personal affront. When we make climbing a part of who we are, it's a small step to making our sociometer's readout dependent on performance. In other words, *our self-worth fluctuates with our performance.* Climbing has become part of our ego.

Describing his first ascent of *Le Reve* (5.14d/5.15a) in Arrow Canyon, Jonathan Siegrist wrote: "It was of course frustrating, ego-crushing, and difficult throughout, but in the end it was a dream come true." Ego-crushing . . . until you succeed!

Self-Relevant Emotions

Let's wrap up psychological science by returning to embarrassment and its friends (shame, humiliation, loneliness, rejection). These are the "self-relevant" emotions in Cooley's Looking Glass Self and Leary's sociometer. I chose to use the term "self-relevant" and many psychologists use "self-conscious," but these terms emphasize just one side of the looking glass—our own. Cooley's mirror is other people. We see ourselves, good or bad, mirrored in the eyes of other people. When they look at us with joy, interest, or admiration, we feel pride. When they laugh at us or look at us with disdain, disgust, contempt, or disappointment, we feel bad (embarrassment, shame, guilt, humiliation, or just plain "bad about myself"). So, these emotions are really about experiences of self-in-relation-to-others. They are triggered by other people and motivate us in ways that are meant to restore or improve other people's evaluations of us.

Leary's gas gauge analogy does a wonderful job of explaining why sensitivity to other people's judgments makes sense. From an evolutionary analysis, we have to be accepted by at least a few people. If our self-esteem and emotions such as guilt were completely dependent on our own self-evaluations and we were completely insensitive to what other people think, then we could delude ourselves into thinking we were god's gift to humanity when in fact everyone else thought we were crap. You may know people like that and I bet you don't look forward to their company. Their sociometer isn't reading accurately, so they drive people away. Their social failures illustrate why the sociometer is adaptive. Leary further explains that a broken sociometer is one way to understand people with certain psychopathologies. The one I just described would be reading full when in fact it was empty, and it describes a narcissist. A gauge that was completely insensitive to others might describe a psychopath.

How can these painful emotions be evolutionary adaptations? Because they motivate us in ways that restore, maintain, or improve our social standing. We apologize or fix things. We avoid doing the "wrong" things. We try to do the "right" things—and do them well! Again, "right and wrong" are subjective. Even silly things like climbing can be the right thing. Then again, when we do poorly, climbing may feel like the wrong thing and we may avoid it or may avoid risking failure.

In case you missed the point, caring about what others think, feeling emotions like embarrassment, and avoiding failure are part of human nature. We all experience these things. It doesn't mean you're not tough or Amerikan. Now we can apply all this science to climbing: how to send more often and have more fun...

The Fear of Failure Plateau

If failure causes embarrassment and embarrassment motivates you to avoid trying hard routes, climbing in front of others, new climbs, new styles of climbing, or new techniques, then fear of failure is holding you back. It is slowing your progress. It is gnawing away at your opportunities to have fun.

Let's say that I consider myself a solid 5.11 climber. One day I go to the crag with my partner, we warm up and he proceeds to climb a classic and cool 5.10+. We are both surprised when he falls repeatedly at the fourth bolt, and again just before the anchors. At the anchors he asks if he should lower, leaving the draws for me to climb the route. In kicks my ego. I know that he usually climbs a little harder than I do, yet he struggled. What if I fall even more times than he did? Why should I risk failing on a 5.10+ when I am a 5.11 climber? I tell him to clean the draws and we go on our way.

Okay, so what's wrong with this picture? First of all, I let my partner's performance affect my motivation to climb a classic route. For all I know, he could be having an off day. The fact of the matter is that my self-image was threatened and I robbed myself of the chance to be challenged. Second, I let my self-imposed 5.11-climber image get in the way.

So, what really happened here? When my self-image, steadfastly protected by my ego, was threatened, I shied away from the challenge that threatened it. I ended the day with my ego intact, but with the niggling and negative thought that I might have failed on a 5.10+ that day. This implies that there may be other 5.10+ climbs out there that I should avoid in similar situations.

Thus, a non-optimal cycle is created or maintained. When I feel like I may fail on a route in the future, I may avoid the climb. Over time, this undermines my experience base and my confidence. I may eventually find myself cherry-picking routes that suit me, which in turn narrows the experience base that I build, further limiting my growth as a rock climber. For most of us, this fear of failure slows our growth as climbers or we may even stagnate in a plateau! In *9 Out of 10 Climbers*, Dave MacLeod emphatically makes the same point about fear of failure. Figure 7.1 illustrates the effect of this negative-feedback system that can hold us back.

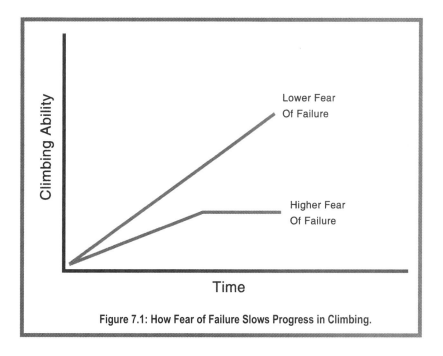

Figure 7.1: How Fear of Failure Slows Progress in Climbing.

Fear of Failure Comes in Many Flavors

Earlier, I referred to research demonstrating the importance evolution has programmed us to place on other people's evaluations of us (i.e., Looking Glass Self). I provided several examples to try to convince you of this. Here I want to take that a step farther, but, more importantly, I want to help you recognize Fear of Failure in all its flavors. These fears are scripted, so by identifying them you can begin to change them.

Psychologists need to measure the things they are studying. So, David Conroy and colleagues developed the Performance Failure Appraisal Inventory. This self-report questionnaire consists of five sections to measure the five flavors of Fear of Failure that they have identified. You can find the PFAI online and take it yourself or you can think about the following explanations. Either way, the intent is to help you identify the B's—Ellis's maladaptive Beliefs in the change process.

The following list presents the five flavors by name and: a) short description; b) a sample item from the PFAI; c) an example from climbing:

1. Fear of Shame and Embarrassment
a. I fear those painful emotions.
b. "When I am failing it is embarrassing if others are there to see it."
c. I felt humiliated when I fell off my warm up.

2. Fear of Devaluing One's Self Estimate
a. I fear I will think less of myself, my self-worth will drop.
b. "When I am failing, I blame my lack of talent."
c. I felt like I couldn't be a real 5.11 climber after falling off that 5.10c.

3. **Fear of Having an Uncertain Future**
   a. My future is threatened because I may not achieve what I want or need to achieve (e.g., rank, status, college degree).
   b. "When I am failing, it upsets my 'plan' for the future."
   c. If I can't redpoint my new project, my sponsors will drop me.

4. **Fear of Losing Social Influence**
   a. People will be less interested in me, less helpful, or won't want to be around me.
   b. "When I am not succeeding, my value decreases for some people."
   c. If I can't climb 5.11, no one will want to climb with me.

5. **Fear of Upsetting Important Others**
   a. People who I value will think less of me.
   b. "When I am failing, important others are disappointed."
   c. If I can't climb 5.11, my girlfriend will think I'm a loser.

Fear of Failure is Social

Fear of feeling bad (embarrassment, shame, low self-esteem) is at the heart of the dysfunctional nature of Fear of Failure in sport. Dysfunctional refers to negative consequences that inhibit performance or fun. Take a few seconds to consider the Looking Glass Self model and the five flavors above. Shame and embarrassment are obviously the major feature of the first component, but the mirror is important too, as most of the questions refer to other people watching or to the negative judgments of other people. In the second flavor, if I think less of myself, then other people probably do too: mirror and negative emotions. Third flavor: My uncertain future is probably not what I'd hoped—more negative self-relevant emotions. Fourth: People won't want to be around me, which is the ultimate threat behind the mirror and shame—social exclusion. Fifth: This is similar to fourth, but now it's worse because they are people I really care about.

In summary, Fear of Failure is all about looking and feeling bad in front of others. Statistical analyses support the central role of embarrassment and shame in Fear of Failure. Again, we may not recognize the Looking Glass Self and related emotions for at least three reasons: 1. Our individualistic culture promotes our lack of awareness; 2. The feelings may be so mild that we don't register them consciously; 3. The emotions may constrict our behavior so that we avoid things that would make us feel them (e.g., trying hard in front of a crowd). In other words, we don't recognize fear of failure because we don't feel those emotions all that often on account of avoiding the risk of looking bad in front of other people and feeling those emotions.

Don't believe these emotions constrict our behavior and motivate us in our choices? Why do you bathe, wash your hair, brush your teeth, or put on deodorant before leaving the house? Are you avoiding something besides rotting teeth? Why do you think twice before you speak? Are there things you'd rather no one knew about you? These are all driven by avoidance. Avoidance, as a script, has important implications for climbing performance and enjoyment.

Negative Effects of Fear of Failure in Sports

I discussed research that described the many varieties of fear of failure. I tried to convince you that it is more common than you might realize. Now, it's time to examine fear of failure and related emotions in sports—in particular, the negative effects—why it is dysfunctional as mentioned previously. Two recent studies found strong evidence that emotions like shame and embarrassment are prevalent among college athletes and that these emotions are strongly related to maladaptive scripts such as fear of failure and perfectionism. A third study, by one of my graduate students, found evidence that when other people (e.g., coaches) trigger athletes' shame and embarrassment, specific negative outcomes follow. The negative effects included trying less hard, dreading practice, thoughts of quitting, anger at self and other people, lowered self-esteem, and decreased motivation.

Some of these consequences of fear of failure are long-term (e.g., quitting), some are short-term (e.g., embarrassment), but most are both (e.g., avoiding practice, de-motivation, anger). The effects on cognition—our ability to think while climbing—are additional short-term consequences that we should all be concerned about. These are immediate effects, in the moment. Recall the discussions of working memory/short-term memory in Chapters 2 and 4. Working memory is closely tied to attention. If you are thinking about your performance, the outcome, how you look to other people, your self-esteem or self-image, then your attention is wasted on the wrong things. Furthermore, you only have so much processing capacity. If you squander it on any or all of these distractions, then your worries will become self-fulfilling prophecies. You will fail!

The Chica Effect/Social Facilitation

So what happens to your performance when other people are watching? Do you shine or do you choke? Or does it depend on the circumstances? The latter is true for most people because having an audience increases arousal, which affects our position on the performance-arousal curve (Chapter 4).

UrbanDictionary.com defines the Chica Effect as "the sudden trance you're put in when a beautiful girl looks you in the eyes." However, a couple of female climbing partners explained it differently: those occasions when a guy suddenly tries to climb harder because an attractive girl is watching. So, my friends and UrbanDictionary focused on the prototypical case of male affected by a female, but it can work in any combination. In the case they describe, the climber dude was low on the performance-arousal curve and the presence of the pretty dudette moved him to the right, increasing arousal, attention, and performance. Psychologists call this social facilitation. Social means audience and facilitate means we do better. In other words, our social natures aren't always bad.

Unfortunately, an audience often has the opposite effect. Let's switch genders. The dudette is at her optimal level of arousal or beyond. Now when the dude walks up, she is pushed too far to the right: arousal increases, focus decreases, and she chokes. This dynamic sounds familiar because we discussed it under the psychology of fear in Chapter 4. Here we are just talking about social fears—how the presence of other people and worrying about our Looking Glass selves affects performance.

The term Chica Effect is revealing, but the scientific research on social facilitation is more general and accurate. Any audience—male or female, attractive or not, friend or foe—may affect us. Performance may increase or decrease. As in Chapter 4, the result is largely dependent on the nature of the task. If it isn't too hard or doesn't require too much precision, you should do better. You can crank the hell out of that warm up you have wired. However, it is more likely to be detrimental on a hard onsight or redpoint.

Coping with Poor Performance

Before discussing Drills and Tactics for addressing maladaptive fear of failure, we need to understand one more piece of the picture. And two pictures will help...

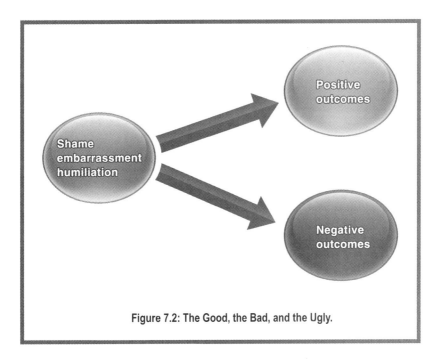

Figure 7.2: The Good, the Bad, and the Ugly.

Embarrassment and related emotions are evolutionary adaptations, but they can lead to positive or negative outcomes. For quite a few years, Figure 7.2 described the state of the research. Researchers investigated the positive outcomes (e.g., trying harder, apologies, avoiding "bad" acts), the negative outcomes (e.g., low self-esteem, depression, anger, avoiding "good" acts), and which emotions (shame vs. guilt) were more maladaptive. My colleagues and I realized that how we cope with these emotions, meaning how we respond, makes an important difference in which types of outcomes we experience (Figure 7.3). For example, one climber may fall, view it as a failure, and be de-motivated, even feel worthless, taking a blow to his self-esteem. In contrast, another climber may take the same fall on the same climb, view it as a challenge or a learning experience, and be more motivated, with her self-esteem unaffected.

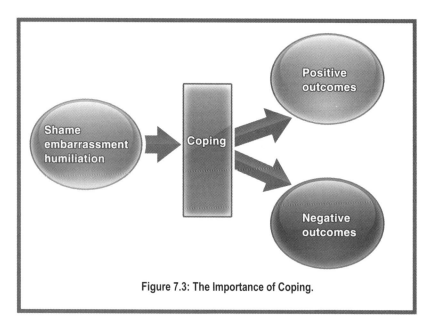

Figure 7.3: The Importance of Coping.

Therefore, coping matters; it makes an important difference. This is what we demonstrated among athletes with regard to fear of failure and perfectionism and all those negative outcomes like anger, trying less hard, and quitting. There are multiple coping styles and some people use bad ones more than good ones. Once again, coping styles are just scripts, and scripts can be identified and changed. So, let's take a quick look at some maladaptive styles you will probably recognize in yourself or others before talking about how to replace them with more helpful, adaptive styles.

The "Compass of Shame"

The Compass of Shame (Figure 7.4) is a model which describes coping styles for the emotions we are talking about. Don't let the word "shame" throw you. Many psychologists, including myself, use it in a very broad way. It's not just some horrible feeling associated with some horrible moralistic failing. Instead, it represents a whole family of emotions: embarrassment, humiliation, hurt feelings, self-disappointment.

The Compass model describes four families of scripts. By "family," we mean there are lots of specific things a person might do that would fall under one of these general families. These styles or families are represented by the poles of the compass and labeled Attack Self, Withdrawal, Attack Other, and Avoidance. You will most likely recognize all of them.

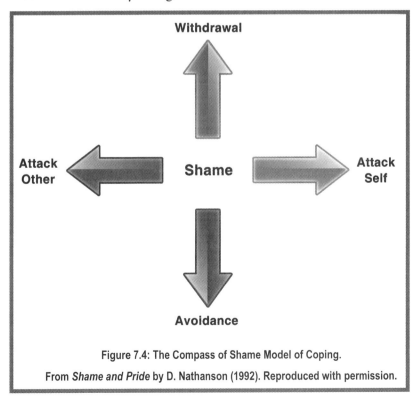

Figure 7.4: The Compass of Shame Model of Coping.
From *Shame and Pride* by D. Nathanson (1992). Reproduced with permission.

At the center of the model, we have some experience that makes you feel bad about yourself: falling, poor performance, bad hair day, wearing Lycra, getting dumped. We then deploy scripts in order to cope with these unpleasant emotions. The four poles of the Compass model describe families of maladaptive scripts we use to reduce, ignore, or even magnify these bad feelings.

In the Withdrawal style, the person acknowledges the experience as negative, accepts that they deserve to feel bad, and tries to withdraw or hide from the situation. For example, a climber falls and just walks away from the crag, without saying a word. They feel bad and they know it. Their thoughts include the belief that they made a bad impression on other people and awareness of their specific faults or shortcomings. Since all these bad thoughts and feelings come from Cooley's Looking Glass Self, they want to escape the mirror. That is to say, they want to get away from the judging eyes of their audience. So, they withdraw, escape, or if trapped, just wish they were invisible.

How many of us have had the perfect climbing record where we've never fallen? How many of us have fallen and wished no one had been there to see it? How many of us have seen another climber walk away from the base of a route, silent, head hung low? That's what I thought.

In the Attack Self style, the person acknowledges the experience as negative, accepts that they deserve to feel bad, and turns anger inward. For example, this time the fallen climber feels self-directed rage for being a Gumby or a loser. In addition to the anger, they are likely to feel contempt or disgust for themselves, which magnifies the impact of the fall. Their thoughts again include the belief that they made a bad impression on other people and awareness of their specific faults or shortcomings. However, they are likely to blow these out of proportion. Instead of realizing that everyone falls, they might think that no real climber would have fallen there. They might think that their fall strips them of self-worth, that they suck. Unlike simple withdrawal, they may not walk away. Their motivation is to make a better impression on others. They might criticize themselves in an effort to elicit sympathy from a partner. They might suck up to others, hoping that adulation might win them acceptance as a groupie or fan. They might train twice as hard to prevent similar failures in the future. That could be good if it works or bad if it results in overtraining and injury.

I'm sure many readers can identify with muttering "I suck" under your breath or thinking: "I'll never get this crux."

In the Avoidance style, the person doesn't usually acknowledge the experience as negative. Instead, they attempt to distract themselves and others from the painful feeling. For example, the fallen climber might joke about it, pretend they don't care, or distract others by bragging about something else. Their thoughts are unlikely to include the belief that they made a bad impression on other people or awareness of their own faults or shortcomings. They are motivated to minimize the conscious experience of embarrassment or show themselves as being above it. Of all the styles, Avoidance scripts are most likely to operate outside of consciousness.

We've all seen these scripts in action. My personal favorite is the speed with which my past climbing record springs to mind (and even lips), reminding myself that I once onsighted the route I just fell off of! My friends reassure me that I'm not a "has-been"—I'm more of a "never-was."

Acknowledging failure in oneself doesn't feel good and requires a lot of humility. Even reading about it can be unsettling. Recalling the ABC process, bringing these hang-ups into consciousness is a necessary step toward improving one's mental game. But it may be one of the hardest steps, since avoidance itself is the struggle.

Finally, in the Attack Other style, the person may or may not acknowledge the experience as negative and attempts to make someone else feel worse. For example, the fallen climber might turn the tables by mocking someone else or they may change feeling bad about themselves to anger and blame the belayer, the bolting job, the weather, or the alignment of the planets. Throwing tantrums—and shoes—helps. Anger at someone or something else is generally more comfortable than feeling bad about ourselves! Attack Other tactics have the added benefit of showing bystanders that you aren't happy or responsible for your performance. You are obviously a better climber than this dismal performance would lead them to believe. Thoughts are focused on blaming someone or something else. The person's motivation is to bolster their image, to others and themselves.

Unless you live in a cave—and climb in one that other climbers don't know about—then you have seen Attack Other in action. I wish I could say I never threw a wobbler...

Ego and Identity

If you can't recognize these coping styles in yourself, fellow climbers, and in daily life, then you aren't paying attention to the world around you. How often do batters yell at the umpire? How often do parents yell at coaches? How about parents yelling at their kids—because their kids' behavior is embarrassing the parent? The fact that we recognize and use all four styles illustrates not just the styles, but another important point discussed above: the role of ego and identity. Parents naturally identify with their kids, so their kids' performances and behaviors reflect on the parents' egos. Similarly, when we identify ourselves as climbers, when it's a big part of who we are, when our self-worth is most dependent on performance, that's when we feel the biggest blows—call them shame, embarrassment, humiliation, disappointment, etc. The stronger the identification or the bigger the ego, the bigger the blow, and the harder we try to cope. That wobbler I mentioned (deceptively using the singular) was when I most identified my self-worth with my performances and when my performances were most visible to others—during the early days of climbing competitions.

Problems are Really Opportunities!

We have presented a long list of problems associated with fear of failure: avoiding challenges that would lead to improvement, dreading practice, thoughts of quitting, anger at self and other people, lowered self-esteem, decreased motivation, perfectionism, loss of focus, and over-arousal. Perhaps you can identify some of these problems in yourself or partners. That may sound like bad news, but by identifying a problem, you have really identified an opportunity—to improve performance and make climbing even more fun.

More good news! These problems are scripted. Scripts are mostly learned. Therefore, they can be unlearned (and replaced).

But wait, there's more good news. You have already learned, and perhaps practiced, the process needed to address these problems by changing scripts.

Recall Ellis's ABC steps:

1. Identify Consequences: falling, plateaus, avoiding challenges, anger, blows to your self-worth, self-criticism.

2. Examine the Antecedents: poor performance, audiences, hinging your self-worth on performance.

3. Identify the underlying Beliefs: People will think I suck if I don't send.

4. Debunk those beliefs: Have you ever been dumped or lost a friend because you fell and handled it gracefully?

Therefore, many of the Drills and Tactics in the next chapter will help you identify the most common scripts involved in fear of failure and coping. We will also examine common maladaptive beliefs and approaches to debunking them. Finally, we will offer more constructive alternatives.

8 Drills and Tactics to Address Fear of Failure

By Jeff Elison

❝ Success is not final, failure is not fatal; it is courage that counts.

— *Winston Churchill*

There are many opportunities to improve climbing performance and increase enjoyment through mental training. Most readers probably bought this book with themselves in mind. Improving your own climbing is the focus of this chapter; however, every tip that helps you may potentially help others: a partner, friend, family member, or significant other. These tips can also help coaches. With that in mind, we split a number of topics between this and the following chapter on co-creative coaching. You will probably benefit from reading both chapters, even if you don't plan to coach others. Just as the tips in the present chapter can be applied to others, many of the tips in the next chapter can be applied to yourself.

Figure 7.3 from the previous chapter suggests two points of intervention for helping yourself (or others):

- Minimize fear of failure/embarrassment and its friends

- Improve coping

How to Use This Chapter

Drills and exercises in this chapter consist of following Ellis's ABC process with our help. In the pages that follow, we list many common scripts involved in fear of failure and coping. The scripts are then followed by questions and answers that help Debunk the irrational Beliefs that underlie the scripts and lead to the maladaptive Consequences. Finally, we will offer more constructive alternatives.

Some of these scripts will apply to you and some may not. We aren't suggesting that you do every drill and exercise in this chapter. Just as you can't follow every training tip simultaneously, you can't address every problematic script simultaneously. So, treat this chapter like a menu. Your job is to identify which maladaptive scripts and Beliefs are most relevant to you. Then consider how we have debunked them. We encourage you to think of additional arguments using Ellis's technique of looking at evidence for and against each belief. We know the Beliefs and Debunking arguments we present apply to many people, but you may be even more effective by customizing them for yourself. In any case, the goal is to latch onto a few convincing reasons why you should think and feel differently and then practice them. We also offer alternative scripts.

Practice involves:

1. Catching yourself in the midst of that maladaptive script. "Darn, there I go again."

2. Reminding yourself why it makes no sense: a quick review of your arguments.

3. Switching to your new, desired script. "OK, I'm not going to continue down this road. I'm going to do XYZ instead."

Many of the exercises that follow specific scripts are meant to help you with one or more of these scripts. For example, one of the most important exercises we present is to be aware of when you decide not to face a challenge. And then ask yourself why.

As we explained in Chapter 2, success requires repetition. You will find that, with repetition, you catch yourself when you are about to use old scripts more quickly: "Oh, I was just about to...". This is progress; don't give up. Progress also entails getting better at following the new script, just like progress in executing a new physical technique. Using your new scripts effectively in more stressful situations (under the gun) is also progress. Eventually, you will skip #2 and won't need to remind yourself why your old scripts are bad. Finally, the whole thing will be automatic, non-conscious. You will have firmly replaced old scripts with new ones.

Ironically, the way we define "success" and "failure" can be a maladaptive script itself. In fact, it is the second irrational Belief we address in the next section. Any progress should represent success. Progress in a new workout is often clear and tangible—I did one more pull-up. But without familiarity, progress in mental training may be less tangible. That's why we explicitly described the types of progress you will see in the previous paragraph. Celebrate the little successes, don't get discouraged, and don't give up. Finally, remember that we all backslide at times, especially when we face that whole "under-the-gun" thing. We may have felt solid with our new scripts and then we find ourselves in some highly stressful situation where we just don't have the mental resources to maintain our new ways. We find ourselves 20 feet above a bolt on slippery footholds, so we revert back to overgripping. Dieters, alcoholics, and those who try to quit smoking know how common it is to slip up. If you beat yourself up for backsliding, you will never get there. Beating yourself up is another maladaptive script that we address. It just de-motivates you. Simply acknowledge your slip and get back on track.

Note that in this chapter we are dealing with fear of failure, so whereas falling was the undesired Consequence in previous chapters, falling/failure can be the Antecedent (cause) or Consequence here. As an Antecedent, failure or thinking about failure is what sets off many of these scripts, leading to negative consequences like de-motivation or feeling worthless. Nevertheless, the added pressure we inflict on ourselves with many of these scripts moves us to the right on the performance-arousal curve and leads to choking, where falling is the Consequence. Additionally, in the long-term view, these scripts operate in cycles and may lead to more falling/failure in the future. In other words, how I deal with today's fall will affect my probability of success in the future by distracting me or de-motivating me.

Minimizing Fear of Failure & Embarrassment

Let's start by putting climbing into perspective. Many maladaptive scripts arise from how we set priorities or value things. We think they are more important than they really are or should be—to ourselves, others, or the world. If I believe that Jean-Claude Van Damme getting snubbed for an Oscar is evidence that there is no justice in the world, I'm likely to be disappointed and angry. Why? In Ellis's words, my anger is an undesirable Consequence of my own irrational Belief. Justice encompasses much more than recognition of this fine (?) actor. We could rightly place many debates regarding climbing ethics in a similar category. Going back to the '70s and '80s, I remember heated debates about chalk, bolts, Friends, sticky rubber, and even sit-starts! Now we laugh at the thought that most of these were controversial.

The general script in this section looks like this: "I feel bad (angry or inferior) when I fall/fail." There are countless variants that follow this form. The immediate Consequence is the bad feeling: anger, inferiority, embarrassment, etc. The longer term Consequences extend much farther, to all the negative outcomes discussed in the previous chapter (e.g., lack of progress, lack of motivation, depression). The bottom line is that if you suffer any of these negative Consequences, then this section applies to you. On the following scale, check (or make a mental note of) the frequency of how often you feel anger, inferiority, or embarrassment after you fall. Which emotions are most common?

Never	Seldom	Sometimes	Often	Almost Always

How important is climbing in the big picture?

Belief: "Climbing is the coolest sport ever, so I have to excel" (and many variations).

Debunk: Face it, climbing is largely a selfish pastime. Don't get me wrong, I love climbing and sometimes it is hard to understand how anyone wouldn't. But climbing benefits me; it gets me out in nature, motivates me to stay in shape, offers me a challenge, and I frequently have fun doing it. It's selfish—in the sense that I'm the one who benefits. Sure, some of us establish routes, maintain routes, help or coach other climbers, but that's mostly just sharing the fun. We don't solve any of the world's problems. We aren't curing cancer, solving global warming, feeding starving children, or promoting world peace. We don't make the world a better place for others, with the minor exceptions noted above.

So, maybe it's not so important that you are the best climber in the world or that you climb 5.13.

Sometimes an explicit reminder before leaving the ground that "it's just climbing" can be extremely effective. Similarly, simplifying the unknown down to "I'll either send or I'll fall—a safe fall," "I'll just try again," can reduce pressure. Believe it or not, simply smiling will help. It may sound corny, but it's true. Usually we smile because we are happy, but we can turn it around and make ourselves feel better by smiling. Without consciously realizing it, our brains correlate smiling with being happy and relaxed. The latter can make this effective at rests. If you are having problems with your location on the performance-anxiety curve (being over-amped), simple tactics like these can really work. There is a whole body of psychological research showing how we can trick ourselves. I used the just-climbing tactic at least a hundred times this past year because it worked.

In spite of the fact that believing climbing is the most important thing in the world is irrational (as are the other beliefs to follow), debunking them doesn't have to be de-motivating. We should be able to enjoy climbing and be motivated, even if it isn't the cure to cancer or doesn't make the Olympics.

How do you define "failure"?

Belief: "If I don't send/onsight this go, I have failed."

Debunk: This line of reasoning has one of the most powerful effects on enjoyment, motivation, and progress. How do you define success and failure? It's all about perspective. This is what some people refer to as framing—how you frame/view/define the experience. Personal definitions and frames are simply scripts—our habitual ways of thinking about things. If you define success too narrowly and failure too broadly, you will by definition (pun intended) fail more often.

> "When trying such a hard long-term project it's really important to find and enjoy the small successes along the way. Maybe it's just a certain feeling of lightness or a small bit of new beta, but if you can find ways to keep progressing then it can continue to be interesting and motivating [emphasis added]."
> - *Chris Sharma describing* La Dura Dura, *thought to be 5.15c (from 8a.nu)*

Definition 1: Define success as progress, mistakes as learning opportunities. Much of this debunking relates to topics covered in Chapter 3 on fun. Climbers who have a mastery orientation and are intrinsically motivated view progress as a process of learning from their mistakes and falls. They celebrate the little successes, as in the quote from Chris Sharma. They may say, "I fell, but I got closer, so I'm improving." Research shows that they learn more quickly, because they look at mistakes and think about what they should be learning, rather than wasting thought on what the mistake says about their self-worth or other people's judgments. They ask: "Why did I fall? What should I do differently in the future?"

Many years ago, after two elbow surgeries for climbing-induced tendonitis, I was slowly regaining fitness. I was nowhere near my previous peak, but I was climbing harder than I thought I might, ever again. I decided to up the ante a bit with a route that was harder than anything I had done in six or seven years. I began redpoint attempts after a few good dogging sessions. It took me eight more tries after my first one-hang burn. But I was having a great time because I loved the route for its movement (intrinsic motivation) and, equally important, each burn made me stronger and got me incrementally closer (mastery orientation). Even though they were small increments—falling off the same handholds, but moving to the next foothold—I felt like every burn was a success. I viewed the whole experience as a process.

In contrast to a mastery orientation, I could have taken a performance orientation and been bummed out by the fact that, at my peak, I probably would have done the climb third go. Or I could have been extrinsically motivated, worrying about whether other people were counting my attempts. Either of those would have been de-motivating and spoiled the experience. Instead, I had fun and got stronger.

Definition 2: Define success as having fun. Some climbers care very little about performance. Others care about performance, but prioritize fun, friendships, partners having fun, and being in nature. It's not hard to find top climbers who don't seem to be having much fun. Some of the best periods I've had climbing have been when I had no expectations about performance. I was either recovering from injuries, out of shape due to life's distractions, or had moved to a new area. I'd rather climb with partners who are having fun, and I'm sure I'm a better partner when I have fun.

Definition 3: Define success as being healthy and able to climb. This one doesn't jump right out at many of us. However, climbers who have been injured repeatedly (sometimes older climbers) often feel more frustration over not being able to climb than they do over sub-optimal performance. Training and trying your hardest come with risks. You might climb your hardest . . . or you might go months away from the crags and climbing walls.

Another benefit of this definition is that it makes it easier to deal with missed workouts. Some of us are fanatical about our training schedules and get frustrated or even angry when life interferes with climbing. However, it can be consoling to think "I won't get injured today" or "Rest makes me stronger" or "Today is a chance for my muscles and tendons to heal."

After three back-to-back injuries so close together that I didn't spend more than five months at a time healthy, I embraced this definition. I started the season slower than I ever had, did minimal physical training, and did not worry about performance. I had a great time and finished the season within two letter grades of my best redpoints and a single letter grade of my best onsights—from when I was 15 years younger!

Definition 4: Define success and failure in terms of tradeoffs. We make hundreds of decisions while climbing and most involve tradeoffs. Should I risk the fall or downclimb and jump? Should I milk this hold to get a better grip or should I just move quickly?

Should I grip harder in case my foot slips or should I conserve strength? Unless you get hurt, it is often difficult to know whether you made the right choice. If we make it to the top, we seldom second-guess these choices. If we fall, many of us chronically second-guess them, even beat ourselves up over them. They become less upsetting when we view them as tradeoffs: "I could only pick one; I don't know that I chose incorrectly." And if I discover I did, then I will learn from it—for this send and maybe future sends.

Exercise: How do you define success? First, answer this in general terms. Then, pick two specific goals, one short-term and one long-term. List all the milestones that you would consider to be successful progress toward those goals:

_____
_____
_____
_____
_____
_____

Who cares about my performance (besides me)?

Belief: "If I don't send/onsight this go, other people will think less of me."

Debunk: Developmental psychologists talk about egocentrism, which is the tendency to see things from our perspective and either fail to imagine other people's perspectives or overrate other people's concern with us. This tendency has a peak during the teen years and so is labeled adolescent egocentrism. The classic example is having a bad hair day or a stain on one's clothes. The adolescent student just knows that "Everyone in school is talking about it"—sometimes referred to as the imaginary audience.

Reality check! Most people either don't care or they are caught up in their own egocentrism, worrying about their hair, clothes, or redpoint. Sure, some of them will feel a little better about themselves if they happen to notice that they did better than you did. However, most people are too focused on their own performance to pay much attention to your falls. Some even break out of their egocentrism and remember what it was like when they fell off that climb or appreciate that you are pushing your limits.

As for non-climbers, most of them don't think climbing is all that cool, important, or impressive. Most of them don't even understand the grading systems or what makes a climb easy or hard. In fact, they might be more impressed when you fall: "Gosh that must be hard…she's so brave…"

Perhaps the worst consequence of this script is avoidance. When we shy away from challenges because of what other people may think, we really limit our progress.

Exercise: For the next few times you go to the gym or crag, notice whether an audience changes your choices or performance. Do you get concerned about what someone else will think if you do poorly? Do you avoid certain routes/problems when other people are around? Do specific people affect you more than others? If so, who?

Exercise: This one may be even more effective at revealing the downside to concern over other people's evaluations of you. Next time you think about taking on a challenge, but decide not to, ask yourself why. Were other people's opinions involved?

The Most Basic Irrational Belief

A quick interlude before continuing: Ellis has found that irrational Beliefs are often nested. For example, "I can't fall." Why is that bad? "Because other people will think I'm a mediocre climber." Why is that bad? "Because they will think less of me." Why is that bad? "Because I will lose their approval." Why is that bad? "Because they will abandon me." Aha! Under all those layers, the most basic fear is the one that evolution has programmed into us: exclusion/abandonment. Remember, if we were cast out of the tribe in days past, we were as good as dead. The threat of abandonment drives fear of failure, shame, embarrassment, and low self-esteem. Playing this script forward: "I have to perform well to gain or maintain approval or else I'm worthless and no one will want to be around me."

Ellis identified a very short list of three basic irrational Beliefs that underlie almost all others. This link between performance and approval may be the most important one on his list. Ultimately, it underlies many of the maladaptive scripts and irrational Beliefs we debunk here, including the one above and the five that follow regarding self-worth, expectations, perfection, and identity. On the following scale, check (or make a mental note of) the frequency of how often you equate your self-worth with performance? In other words, how frequently do you feel good about yourself when you succeed and bad about yourself when you fall short of expectations?

Never	Seldom	Sometimes	Often	Almost Always

Although we offered several arguments to Debunk the idea that other people are all wrapped up in our performances, we could have continued. If the link between performance and approval is driving your maladaptive scripts by underlying your irrational Beliefs, then we could Debunk that one too. Do your friends, family, loved ones accept you and approve of you in spite of your shortcomings? Have any of them ever rejected you because you failed to send? Is climbing the only thing that defines your self-worth? Do you have any other redeeming qualities? Hopefully these sound silly. They should.

Is my self-worth dependent on my performance?

Belief: "If I don't send/onsight this go, I suck, I'm worthless."

Debunk: We hit this one hard in the previous paragraph. It is incredibly easy to fall into the trap (script) of equating our self-worth with our performance. It is easy, in part, because parents, siblings, friends, partners, teachers, and coaches praise us when we do well and may not (or worse) when we do poorly or behave "badly." However, most of them love, like, or respect us in spite of our shortcomings. Those who don't may have poor parenting/coaching/friend skills, or they may just be lousy people.

Remember Cooley's Looking Glass Self. Sometimes the mirror is a fun-house mirror, one like you see at county fairs. They reflect a distorted image. Some people are just like those mirrors—they reflect a distorted image. I wouldn't have a mirror like that in my house, so why would I want a friend or partner like that?

Because this irrational Belief underlies many of the other irrational Beliefs presented here, the Debunking arguments for those Beliefs apply to this one and vice versa. So, let's continue on, looking at expectations, mistakes, and identity. Realize that if you are still shaky on Debunking this one, the following arguments will help.

Exercise: You have countless people serving as Cooley's looking glasses, people whose judgments affect you. Which ones reflect a warped image? The fact that they reflect a warped image is enough to discount their importance. Can you think of other reasons?

_____

_____

_____

_____

_____

Is my self-worth relative to others' performance?

Or, "John Doe onsighted, so I suck if I don't."

Belief: "My worth as a human being is determined by my rank among fellow climbers."

Debunk: Psychologists call this *social comparison* and have studied it extensively. It presents another dangerous trap that we step into so easily because it is natural. However, some of us buy into it more than others. It relates to intrinsic and extrinsic motivation: Am I doing this for myself or for others? Is climbing in and of itself enjoyable to me? Motivation is one aspect, but there's much more to this Belief.

We all want to have high self-esteem or self-worth—a full sociometer tank. When the tank is low or leaky, it's natural to make efforts to fill it up. An obvious way to do this is to look around until you find someone with whom to make a favorable comparison. "Well, I know I'm better than him," whatever "better" means (e.g., looks, climbing, income). Research shows the dangers of this game.

First, don't you have worth simply because you are a human being? Don't our laws, religions, and social conventions tell us that everyone is equal? So, when you tell yourself you are "better" in order to bolster your self-worth, you are really saying the other person is less worthy. You feel better by demeaning others. Not only is this not cool, you are saying not everyone has the same worth. If that's the case, then there must be other people out there who are more worthy than you.

Second, we are complicated beings, with hundreds of attributes. Although you may climb better than him, he may have done something important, like saved lives. Although she climbs better than you, she may be a ditz or just plain mean. I've met plenty of top climbers who I would never want to emulate.

Third, hanging your self-worth on relative performance is a short-term fix that is guaranteed to backfire. You may be a badass today, but 12-year-old climbers will warm up on your projects 30 years from now. Unless you end up in the Climbers Hall of Fame, few people will remember your climbing record. Moreover, you won't be sending at that grade forever. What then? Will you be devoid of self-worth, or will you just find some other favorable domain in which to tell yourself you are better than others?

Fourth, research backs your mom when she said: "When you point your finger at someone, your other three fingers are pointing back at you." You judging them just serves as an example, more confirmation, that people judge each other. You open the door to being less worthy because you just set the precedent: It's okay for better climbers to judge you. So, unless you are Chris Sharma, there is always someone better than you, someone to point down at you. Ondra who? Oh yeah, point made!

Exercise: The next time you go climbing, notice the comparisons you make with others. Do they happen automatically? If so, you can change this script. Every time you catch yourself making a comparison, whether favorable ("I did that quicker") or unfavorable, stop and think back to the debunking arguments from the previous four points that work best for you.

Exercise: Note how often grades and accomplishments come up in your conversations with others, climbers and non-climbers. These conversations can make you feel good when you've had a good day and bad when things haven't gone well. Take a little break from this sort of talk. Consciously avoid offering or soliciting information about grades and performance. See how taking a break makes you feel.

Exercise: Social comparisons often show up in the fine art of bragging. Dan McMillan wrote a brilliant article called "The Protocol of Boasting" for *Climbing Magazine* back in 1984, which captures the social comparisons so familiar to climbers: tick lists (career or today's list), recommending climbs (especially sandbagging), comparing an easier route someone mentions to a much harder route you have done, and rating climbs ("No way that's 12a; it can't be harder than 11c"). For this exercise, deploy some of Dan's recommended defensive strategies. When someone asks you what you climbed today, they often don't care; they just want to tell you what they did. You can deflect the brag-fest by responding with disinterest: "Climbed" or "some stuff over there." Or you can feign ignorance when they tell you about their feats: "Oh, *The Naked Edge*, that's 5.9, right?" (when in reality it is a classic multi-pitch 5.11 trad route). Or the opposite approach can make their feats appear less amazing: "Wow, you sent a 13a," making them reply, "No, *Goldfinger* is only 12a." Have some fun with this exercise and it really will help you reduce social comparisons.

Do I have to be perfect?

Belief: "If I make mistakes, other people will think less of me."

Debunk: We'll keep this one short and to the point because we will address perfectionism as a larger script in a few pages. No one is perfect. Everyone makes mistakes. Last summer I onsighted a notorious Rifle 12b that some 5.14 climber fell on multiple times. Do I think I'm a better person than he is? Of course not. Do I think he is a better person? Of course not. I think he is a better climber, I had a great day, he had a bad day. Sounds realistic.

A really effective strategy to deal with this irrational Belief is to ask yourself, "Okay, since everyone makes mistakes, how many mistakes are acceptable?" If you are a perfectionist, "none" may be your automatic answer. But how many mistakes do you allow other people before you turn your back on them? If you are a decent human, it is probably at least a few. So, be decent to yourself. Allow yourself a few mistakes, falls, whatever per day or week. Doing this can have amazing effects. You won't turn into an unmotivated slacker, and you won't beat yourself up for each and every mistake. In fact, by the end of the week, you may lose track: "Did I make two or three? I don't remember, but it was a pretty good week anyway."

Exercise: Before you even start your week, pick a number of mistakes that you will allow yourself. Now, you aren't allowed to get mad or disappointed with yourself until you exceed that number during the upcoming week.

What do I or others expect?

Do I have to live up to others' expectations?

Belief: "If I fall, I fall short of expectations—mine or other people's."

Debunk: Years ago, I worked as a software engineer for Intel. At the time (and maybe currently), they embraced MBO (Management By Objectives). Managers and their underlings at all levels would agree on the objectives to be met each month by the underling. Interestingly, they thought it was more motivating for everyone to shoot high. So, if you had established a "proper" set of objectives, you should only make about 80 percent. We often do the same as climbers. If we enjoy pushing our limits, we push to falling.

Shooting high can be a double-edged sword. Too much failure is de-motivating and can be un-fun. Too little failure indicates you would probably progress faster or achieve more if you pushed a little harder. Is 80% the right number? Yes and no—it depends on you! Who am I to judge? Who is anyone else to judge? I don't know your goals and priorities, and neither does anyone else: fun vs. performance; safety vs. thrills; injury avoidance vs. big numbers. So, don't let other people set expectations for you. And don't blindly accept them. What are your priorities? Have you thought about them explicitly? Doing so may help you set expectations that are most likely to lead to achieving your goals, whether they are about performance, fun, or both.

I got sucked into doing climbing comps shortly after indoor comps came to the U.S. They looked appealing. They were all over the mags. People were becoming "famous." I enjoyed a few of those experiences, and a few brought out some decent performances—for me personally, not in comparison to the rest of the field. After spending too many dollars on entries and travel, too many hours in isolation listening to too many battling egos, I realized I wasn't having all that much fun. The ROI (return on investment) seemed low. It forced me to explicitly examine my priorities and goals. I realized that climbing real routes, on real rock, in real nature was way more fun and meaningful to me. Win-win situation, I had more fun and ticked more goals.

A byproduct of those competition experiences was a new appreciation for the effects other people's expectations have on us. I was far enough down in the ranks of the comp circuit that no one expected anything from me. However, I had a good friend who was one of the best competitors in the U.S. at the time. She and everyone else came to expect that she would finish in first or second place. The power of expectations hit me when she came in 4th at a national comp. Had it been me at the time, everyone would have said: "What the heck?" I would have been overjoyed, filled with pride. Instead, everyone said: "What happened to her?" She was devastated, depressed, self-deprecating: "I suck; maybe I won't do comps anymore."

Just as setting our own expectations poorly can be dangerous. Other people's expectations can be a problem. You can think of them in terms of that fun-house mirror I described. You can also think of them in terms of a scary metaphor from psychologist Karen Horney: the Tyranny of the Shoulds. We all grow up with people telling us how we should act and who we should be. When we internalize the wrong, unrealistic "shoulds," they create a tyranny, a cruel and oppressive set of rules that crushes us and leads to unhappiness, if not psychological problems.

Exercise: Let's start easy and build up. Can you identify unrealistic expectations that other people have for you? Can you identify unrealistic expectations you have for yourself? Can you identify personal goals that were imposed on you by other people? These may have been explicitly stated or merely implied by other people's reactions or comments. If you can list any, then take some time to reconsider their validity. Do you really need to buy into them?

_____

_____

_____

_____

_____

_____

Is there more to me than just being a climber (Identity)?

Belief: "If I'm not a climber, I'm nothing."

Debunk: Constructing an identity for yourself can be a tricky and dangerous business. It can go wrong in many ways.

First, if your identity doesn't fit you, if it represents those "shoulds" that Horney wrote about, then you may end up unhappy. You may end up feeling trapped (e.g., wrong job, wrong marriage). It even leads some people to an identity crisis or midlife crisis.

Second, even if you choose for yourself, the research reviewed in Chapter 3 shows that we are poor at affective forecasting, predicting what will make us happy. We all want to be rich and famous or win the lottery . . . until it happens and we see the downside first-hand.

Third, what happens if you lose a piece of that identity? Say you move to Guam or grow old or get injured? Research in sports psychology reveals the mental struggles athletes face (e.g., shame, embarrassment, depression) when injured. The problem for many isn't just that they can't do what they love, it's that they lose their identity and therefore their sense of self-worth.

Fourth: Climbing is fun. Climbing is rewarding. Climbing is cool. But hopefully you aren't so one-dimensional that nothing else about you warrants merit. Do you do anything else? Do you have friends, kids, a significant other, other family? Do you have a job? If climbing is all you have in life, you might want to think about the future and find some balance.

I don't mean to be judgmental. At the peak of my addiction, when I met new people, I would identify myself as a climber—before mentioning I was married or a software engineer. At the peak of my addiction, I was climbing harder than I do now, and I was much less happy!

> **Exercise:** In addition to being a climber, what other important characteristics, goals, activities, and relationships make up your identity? In what ways do you expect your identity to change over the next 5, 10, and 20 years?
>
> _____
> _____
> _____
> _____
> _____

Does this single performance change my future?

Belief: "I have to send/onsight this go."

Debunk: Or what? Some of your potential answers probably appeared above and hopefully we have minimized their sting. Why else? Sponsors? Fame? Fortune? Those aren't an issue for the vast majority of us. In addition, sponsors, fame, and fortune bring expectations and pressures that can make climbing feel like a j-o-b, more work than pleasure.

Why else? So, you can move onto your next project? Why is that important? Aren't you enjoying this one? Or are you more concerned with building your tick list?

> **Exercise:** The next time you feel pressure to send on your next attempt, ask yourself: Why am I feeling pressure?
> _____
> _____
> _____
> _____
>
> **Exercise:** The next time you feel stuck on a project, ask your-self: What are the pros and cons of sticking with this route?
> _____
> _____
> _____
> _____

Why else do we feel pressure to send and move on? Because we are tired of the climb, don't like the moves, it's painful, or each burn takes so much effort. See next Belief…

Why does it have to be so hard/scary/painful?

Belief: "This shouldn't be so hard/scary/painful/so much work."
Debunk: Hey, you signed up for this. One, you chose to be a climber. You could take up golf, have a pot-belly, and still drink a beer on every hole. Two, you chose this climb, so you can un-choose it and walk away. Would that be defeat? Would that make you less of a person? If so, revisit the previous irrational Be-liefs. Three, would you really be happy if it weren't challenging? Would climbing be so rewarding if it were easy? Four, if this is too hard, scary, painful to the point where you aren't having fun, then re-examine your priorities. You might be happier and even progress faster by choosing easier routes. Climbers who spend

every day warming up on the same warm ups in order to fail on the same project week-after-week are slowing their progress. I'm not sure how much fun they are having either. You can actually get weaker, physically and mentally, with this approach. Adam Ondra has made this same observation, noting that you get weaker because you spend so much time resting and you only practice such a limited set of moves.

Exercise: Weigh your priorities versus the specific goals you have chosen (e.g., a particular trip or route). What are your priorities: fun, progress, injury prevention, being outdoors, or friends? To what extent do fear, difficulty, challenge, falling, and pain play a role in these priorities? Now, reevaluate your specific goals. Is this route a good match for me, given my priorities and what makes my climbing enjoyable? For example, remember Todd Skinner's quote about flash ascents. He enjoyed the mental and physical challenges of hard redpoints. But you may not.

_____

_____

_____

_____

Self-Compassion: Desirable Scripts

We haven't covered every imaginable irrational Belief behind the negative Consequences of fear of failure and embarrassment, but we have covered a wide range. We have listed Beliefs and arguments to help you Debunk them. Sometimes this is enough— just stop banging your head against the wall and you will feel better. However, we can do better than just stopping. We often need to replace old scripts with something better. What we discuss in this section applies to the scripts and beliefs above, as well as to helping others and addressing coping, discussed later.

Most of my research has been on coping with negative evaluations, mistakes, performance failures, moral failures, faux pas, and rejection that result in shame, guilt, embarrassment, humiliation, and hurt feelings. Fun stuff! I described the model I used for much of this research, the Compass of Shame, in the previous chapter. I developed the Compass of Shame Scale (CoSS), a self-report questionnaire, to measure coping in order to study it. The CoSS has been translated into at least 10 other languages and used in dozens of studies. Its focus is maladaptive scripts, exactly what we have been talking about here. However, researchers often asked me about adaptive coping. Don't we care about the good stuff too? In response, I developed an Adaptive Scale to include in the CoSS. Honestly, the new Adaptive Scale is okay, but it is short and pales in comparison to the research on Self-Compassion.

Self-Compassion is a powerful construct, with some Eastern influences. It is also a multi-dimensional construct, meaning it has multiple components. Just as I developed the CoSS so that maladaptive coping could be studied, Kristin Neff developed the Self-Compassion Scale to measure and study the multiple components of self-compassion. What follows is a list of the three components with a short description of each and examples from her questionnaire of: a) each positive component; and b) its opposite, a negative component:

1. **Self-Kindness:** Acknowledge and accept negative outcomes as real (if they are real). Don't ignore or exaggerate them. Don't beat yourself up over mistakes.
    a. **Example:** "I'm tolerant of my own flaws and inadequacies."
    b. **Counter-example (Self-Judgment):** "When I see aspects of myself that I don't like, I get down on myself."

2. **Common Humanity:** We all suffer, we all fail, we all make mistakes. We are not isolated and alone in our problems.

       a. Example: "When I feel inadequate in some way, I try to remind myself that feelings of inadequacy are shared by most people."

       b. Counter-example (Isolation): "When I fail at something that's important to me, I tend to feel alone in my failure."

3. **Mindfulness:** Focus on the present moment, the task at hand. Don't over-identify with outcomes, keep things in perspective.

       a. Example: "When I fail at something important to me, I try to keep things in perspective."

       b. Counter-example (Over-Identification): "When I'm feeling down, I tend to obsess and fixate on everything that's wrong."

Each of these parts is a family of scripts, just like the families represented by the Compass of Shame. In other words, there are many specific scripts that achieve each of these three larger scripts.

These self-compassion scripts are one very good answer to the question: "With what should I replace my old scripts?"

Research backs the effectiveness of self-compassion. Correlational research shows that people who tend to approach negative events and failures with self-compassion are happier and healthier. They are also more likely to have the types of scripts we, as climbers, want: higher mastery motivation and lower fear of failure. Experimental research demonstrates causality; when subjects are given instruction in self-compassion, they have more positive outcomes. For example, remember my warning at the beginning of this chapter about backsliding while replacing old scripts. College women with eating issues who received instruction in self-compassion felt less distress and ate less after researchers had them eat an unhealthy meal (i.e., backslide) in comparison to those who had not had the self-compassion training.

Compassion is defined as "sympathetic pity and concern for the sufferings or misfortunes of others." Most people expect us to be capable of sympathy. In other words, we should care for others who are suffering or feeling badly. So, shouldn't we be compassionate toward ourselves too?

The descriptions of Self-Kindness, Common Humanity, and Mindfulness above give you some ideas for how you can be compassionate toward yourself. Let's look at them in more detail. The examples and counter-examples are from Neff's Self-Compassion Scale, a self-report questionnaire. So, they give us ideas of what we shouldn't be doing and what we should be doing instead.

For example, imagine you have been working on your project every weekend for the last month. You mentally rehearsed the beta twenty times this past week, you trained hard early in the week, you rested Thursday and Friday. You feel ready, almost sure you will send on Saturday . . . but you don't! What you don't want to do is the opposite of Self-Kindness: Self-Judgment. Self-Judgmental responses would be losing patience with yourself, beating yourself up mentally, telling yourself you suck or you are worthless. Instead, with Self-Kindness you would be understanding about the outcome, patient that maybe you need more time or rest, and you would be able to enjoy a beer with friends around the campfire—self-worth intact! Oh, and your friends would be able to enjoy you—you would be more fun to be around because Self-Kindness isn't wallowing in self-pity.

Extending this same example, the opposite of Common Humanity is Isolation. The latter, to-be-avoided responses include feeling cut-off or isolated from other people, believing that they are happier or their lives are easier. Instead, you could respond in terms of Common Humanity—either all of humanity or just your commonality with other climbers. You would realize that difficulties are part of climbing and all climbers face them. You would remember that lots of other climbers didn't send today. If feelings of inadequacy are gnawing at you, you would remind yourself that they gnaw at everyone.

Finally, the opposite of Mindfulness is Over-Identification. You don't want your mind to be fixated on that one goal, consumed by what the day's outcome means for your self-worth, blowing outcomes out of proportion. Instead, keep some perspective: It's just climbing; you will send it eventually. Approach the outcome with curiosity and openness. Constructively ask yourself what you could have done differently, so you learn from it.

Self-Compassion is a relatively new area of study in psychology, but the research is very promising. Several books have already been published on the topic. If you think learning more about it will help you in terms of performance, happiness, or self-esteem, check out: *Self-Compassion* (Neff, 2011); *The Compassionate Mind* (Gilbert, 2010); *The Mindful Path to Self-Compassion* (Germer & Salzberg, 2009)

> **Exercise:** The next time you feel badly about failing to achieve some climbing goal, note your response in terms of these self-compassion dimensions. Do you blow it out of proportion, or do you keep it in proper perspective? Do you feel isolated in your failure, or do you remind yourself that others have done the same? Do you get caught up in self-criticism, or do you show yourself self-compassion? This exercise can be applied to other situations besides climbing. If you are unhappy with your response to the situation, can you replace some of those problem scripts?

Mindfulness Revisited

There is more to mindfulness than the short description above. Mindfulness encompasses other "Zen-like" aspects. In Lynn Hill's *Free Climbing the Nose* video, Lynn said: "I practiced an attitude of acceptance. No matter what the situation, I made an effort to remain patient and relaxed." Her attitude exemplifies the acceptance aspect of mindfulness described by Neff. However, another big component of mindfulness is the idea of living in the moment, being focused on the now. Psychologists measure people's tendencies to perseverate and ruminate, both of which are counter to mindfulness. To persevere is to stick with something (often good), but perseveration is when your mind is stuck. You can't think about anything else; you aren't living in the now. Similarly, rumination is what I was referring to previously when we incessantly beat ourselves up. We replay our mistakes and flaws over and over. We aren't living in the now, we are living in the past, making the now hell. Rumination is associated with neuroticism, pessimism, low self-esteem, and depression.

Perseveration and rumination are part of Neff's Mindfulness opposite, Over-Identification. As discussed previously, we often over-identify when we make something like climbing too important to our self-image, and when we make our self-worth contingent on performance. All these are dangerous, counter-productive scripts. Instead, we can be mindful by focusing on the moment—appreciating what is going on right now, putting the past in perspective, letting the past go. Tell yourself: "Past is past, time to move forward." Failure to do so will literally hold you down.

The consequences of Over-Identification, perseveration, and rumination are long-term negative effects including those listed in the previous chapter: less enjoyment, poorer performance, trying less hard, dreading training, thoughts of quitting, anger at self and other people, lowered self-esteem, drops in motivation, fear of failure, and perfectionism. However, mindfulness also has direct, immediate effects on performance because of its impact on working memory/short-term memory. So, it's helpful to think of mindfulness in its more "Zen-like" fashion, as well.

Working memory has a very limited capacity. You can only focus on a few things while climbing. Being mindful means living in the moment, focused on the now: "How should I do this move?" "This is how I do it precisely." If you are perseverating or ruminating on past climbs or even moves you should have done better lower on the route, then you are wasting thinking capacity. Similarly, if you are looking ahead at the wrong things— "What if I don't send?," "I've done the crux, I'd better not blow it now," "If I don't send, I'll have to come back next weekend," or even "It's in the bag"—then you are wasting thinking capacity. Worry is especially problematic because it involves two parts: thoughts that distract you from the task at hand, and anxiety that moves you along the performance curve.

> **DRILL:** Attention is like a spotlight. It illuminates a circle of space and time. Visualize your attention as your own personal spotlight. Practice making it illuminate now! Focus all your attention on what you are doing at the moment. That doesn't mean you don't use it to scan ahead. Of course good climbers plan ahead. While at a rest, "now" involves consciously relaxing and recovering, but it can also include scanning ahead.

You can take this visualization a step farther by thinking about climbing by headlight in the dark. Nothing exists outside the circle of light. All you have is what is right in front of you at this moment in time.

Your mind will stray. But being mindful means minimizing the straying by not taking the time to judge these lapses. Let it go, don't beat yourself up, just get back on task. This re-focusing without judgment is integral to meditation.

DRILL: Let's focus the attention spotlight down to a fraction of a second—latching that next hold. The crux. What is in your mind? If self-doubt, worry, or any of the scripts we've discussed previously are in there, then you aren't completely focused. If that's a problem for you, you might want to experiment with using a kiai. A kiai is that forceful expulsion of air, like a yell, often heard at the moment of contact in martial arts. It amps you up, focuses energy, and perhaps most important, it focuses attention by driving out all other thoughts. When I kiai, nothing else exists except me and that move. Maybe not even the whole move—my world comes down to just latching the hold. Try it. Experiment. New things take practice, so give it a fair chance.

By the way, if you are afraid you will sound silly or draw attention to yourself, what is stopping you? That's right: embarrassment, fear of other people's evaluations. Once again, these troublesome emotions are blocking performance.

Improve Coping

We've provided drills and exercises to help you with mindfulness and focus, and now we'll move onto ways to improve your coping. In Chapter 7, we described four ways that we cope with mistakes and failure: the Compass of Shame model. It includes four styles: Attack Self (internalizing feelings of anger and blame), Withdrawal (the tendency to hide or withdraw), Attack Other (externalizing feelings of anger and blame), and Avoidance (the tendency to minimize the importance of negative feelings). Each of these styles represents a family of maladaptive scripts that have negative Consequences. They represent scripts we don't want and should change.

What should we do? With what should we replace them? Self-Compassion is one answer. A second answer is to treat the experience (e.g., embarrassment) as information and deal with it. This could mean learning from the experience, fixing any problems, or realizing that your feelings stem from viewing yourself in a warped Looking Glass. In the latter case, other people have unrealistic expectations, different priorities, or misconceptions. Therefore, you don't need to feel bad and hopefully the feelings dissipate more quickly. All of these alternative responses are more adaptive than the Compass scripts. To help you identify maladaptive coping and motivate you to replace those scripts, let's take another look at each family. Again, the "drill" here is to recognize which scripts apply to you, their negative Consequences, and how they can be replaced. You can do this to help yourself or other people.

The negative Consequences from all four coping styles include poorer performance, de-motivation, and less enjoyment, as in the study of college athletes and coaches described in the previous chapter. More specifically, think about Attack Other. Attack Other indicates you are over-identified with climbing or specific outcomes. If you blame other people and other causes for your mistakes, if you vent your anger at your belayer or the gods, then you might expect to lose partners. You aren't a lot of fun to climb around. I mentioned throwing shoes earlier. Another downside to "venting" your anger is that it doesn't usually work—you don't feel less angry afterward. The Catharsis Hypothesis predicts that yelling and throwing things releases your anger so you will calm down. Nope, research does not support this one. In fact, you are likely to get angrier and be upset for a longer period of time. So, you might be happier and better-off by viewing your "failure" and reaction from this broader perspective.

Have you ever been frustrated when repeated attempts didn't yield success? Yeah, me too! Merriam-Webster's dictionary defines frustration as: "a deep chronic sense or state of insecurity and dissatisfaction arising from unresolved problems or unfulfilled needs." There are two interesting aspects to this definition. First, we chose to face most of our "unresolved problems" in climbing. We just get frustrated when they take longer than we expected. Second, note the "insecurity" over "unfulfilled needs." Frustration, especially in climbing, has ego written all over it. The unfulfilled need is to bolster, or at least protect, our egos by seeing ourselves in a positive light, by living up to our own and others' expectations.

Think of it this way: If we love climbing so much, then what's the problem with making lots of attempts? Expectations, ego, and self-worth. Frustration is a component of Attack Other scripts, exacerbated by over-identification. We set expectations based on our self-assessment ("I should send this route in three or four tries."). When our self-assessments turn out to be wrong ("Damn, this will be my tenth attempt."), our egos and self-worth feel threatened. Threats and emotional discomfort (e.g., fear of failure, fear of negative evaluation, embarrassment) trigger anger-based frustration.

So, how can we minimize Attack Other and frustration? One, reduce over-identification (an irrational belief) with some of the debunking arguments we offered earlier. Two, minimize expectations. Approach challenges with an open mind. Three, reframe success as progress. Four, focus on the other rewards: fun moves, learning, friends, the natural setting.

Now think about Attack Self, in which you get angry at yourself, feel self-loathing, or ruminate about your mistakes. Research that my colleagues and I have conducted demonstrates that Attack Self is closely related to Self-Compassion. Attack Self is virtually identical to the Self-Judgment component of the Self-Compassion Scale and it predicts lower levels of Self-Kindness. It is what psychologists call intropunitive or self-punishing. In addition, Attack Self involves magnifying the meaning, significance, and emotions surrounding the mistake. Because of the magnification and self-punishing, we have repeatedly found that Attack Self most strongly predicts psychological problems: neuroticism, low self-esteem, depression, fear of failure, and perfectionism. Few of us enjoy being punished by parents, teachers, or the law, so do you really need to punish yourself for merely falling?

The downsides of Withdrawal are pretty clear: You either quit climbing because you have ruined it for yourself or you limit progress because you want to escape after every poor performance. In our studies, Withdrawal runs a close second to Attack Self when it comes to predicting many negative outcomes (e.g., low self-esteem, depression).

Avoidance coping comes in many flavors, but when we use it, we are basically either distracting ourselves and others from our shortcomings, or we are pretending like we don't care/our goals don't matter. The problem here is the pretending and distracting aspects. We are neither acknowledging the problem, nor putting things into perspective. We might say: "Climbing isn't that important to me" or "Climbing isn't really fun," but we aren't being honest. I enjoy a beer at least as much as the next guy, but with Avoidance we might be dousing our real reactions with alcohol or other drugs. We might be bragging about other achievements (climbing or beyond) in order to soothe ourselves. In any case, we might fool ourselves by pretending and, as a result, be de-motivating ourselves. We might also avoid challenges that would help us improve. Rather than risk failure, we avoid it.

Another Avoidance ploy is *self-handicapping*, in which we pre-justify or rationalize a lack of effort or poor performance. "On belay? Oh, did I mention I drank an entire fifth of gin single-handedly last night . . . so don't expect too much from me." "This is my 19th day on, I worked the night shift, and my girlfriend dumped me." Self-handicapping has the benefits (?) of setting other people's expectations low, reducing embarrassment, and protecting our egos, but it has a serious downside. We are setting our own expectations low and we may just live up to them in a self-fulfilling prophecy of poor performance. Furthermore, self-handicapping is associated with less learning, lower persistence, lower intrinsic motivation, poorer health and well-being.

Perfectionism

The main purpose in this chapter was to decompose problems into the tiniest, lowest-level scripts and beliefs, in order to debunk and change them. However, there are some larger scripts that apply to sports performance because they include aspects of fear of failure and coping. Two of these are self-efficacy and perfectionism. We will discuss perfectionism here and self-efficacy in the next section.

Scripts can be very complex with many components, a larger script consisting of many smaller ones. A classic example is going to a good restaurant. You have a script for being greeted and seated, a script for ordering, a script for eating, and a script for paying. Do you use the seat-yourself script, or the server-seats-us script, or the host-seats-us script? What if you had great versus horrible service? All these scripts may vary depending on the restaurant (McD's vs. a five-star steakhouse) and players' specific behaviors (e.g., rude server). You get the idea.

One of these large scripts is *perfectionism*. The multiple, component scripts of perfectionism are illustrated by Robert Hill's Perfectionism Inventory, which uses 59 items to assess the following seven components:

- Overly upset about mistakes
- Rumination: replaying mistakes over and over...
- Need for approval: "Did I do good?"
- High standards for others
- Organization
- Planfulness
- Striving for excellence

Interestingly, perfectionism is a mixed bag of positive and negative scripts. Having high standards, striving for excellence, being organized and well-planned can be very positive. In fact, many university departments and businesses look for these things in potential students and employees. Some go so far as to seek perfectionists. However, all of these can become too extreme. Having overly high standards for other people makes you a critical pain in the ass. Even overly high standards (i.e., unrealistic expectations) for yourself set you up for failure and disappointment. Specifically, expecting perfection (e.g., flawless performance) is delusional. If you want to be a better climber, you have to push your limits. If you push your limits, you will fall. If you can't accept falls because of your need for perfection, then you can't push your limits and you won't make progress (or it will be much slower). Similarly, if you spend more time and concern on planning and organization than you do on execution and living your life, they may paralyze you and inhibit your progress.

The other aspects of perfectionism are more obviously maladaptive. Blowing mistakes out of proportion so that they derail your efforts and spoil your (and others') day don't lead to happiness or progress for anyone. We have already discussed Rumination as a component of Attack Self coping and a lack of Self-Compassion. Finally, an overly high need for approval indicates you are hinging your self-worth on other people's opinions, which leads us back to most of the fear of failure scripts, beliefs, and debunking arguments.

The basic message is to find a happy medium, a balance in all these areas. There is a difference between neurotic, obsessive perfectionism and normal perfectionistic tendencies. Plan, but don't over-plan. Have high, but realistic expectations…

Perfectionists can be a pain in the ass. I grew up around a few and qualified as one myself. At some point, I realized it wasn't fun. I now joke with my students that I'm a "semi-reformed perfectionist" and use this to explain the two main points above: one, seek balance; two, there are adaptive and maladaptive aspects of perfectionism. Embrace the former in moderation, and drop the latter. So, once again, set realistic expectations, don't beat yourself up, and don't hinge your self-worth solely on other people's approval. At the same time, plan, be organized, and try to do well.

Sounds so simple! The "semi-reformed perfectionist" line is only half joking. You can adopt those attitudes without turning into a worthless slacker. Most "reformed perfectionists" are still organized, well-planned, and perform well. The real reform is that we are much happier than we used to be!

Self-Efficacy

Self-efficacy is basically the belief that you can be successful within a specific domain (e.g., climbing or statistics). It encompasses a large set of scripts, including aspects of fear of failure and coping, and it has important implications for climbing performance. Climbers with higher self-efficacy climb harder (on average). Recall Russ Raffa's comment about Lynn Hill way back in 1987: Some people expect success 50% of the time when faced with a crux; the other half of the time, they are expecting to fall (paraphrased). "In Lynn's case, it's 98% one way, 2% the other."

For starters, self-efficacy has important motivational effects that apply directly to climbing:

1. It affects your choice of behaviors.
    a. High: "I'm going to try to redpoint a letter grade harder than ever before because I believe I can do it."
    b. Low: "Why bother trying it, I won't make it."
2. It affects effort and persistence.
    a. High: "I know I can get it eventually, so I'll train hard and keep trying."
    b. Low: "I don't know if I'll ever get it. I'm de-motivated, so I'll give up."
3. It affects learning and achievement.
    High: "I learn more and achieve more because I push my limits, try harder, and persist—because I believe in my abilities."
    Low: "Because I don't try anything hard, put in much effort, or persist when the going gets tough, I learn and achieve less."

When I teach the principles of self-efficacy in Developmental Psychology or Motivation and Emotion, I always use climbing videos to illustrate them. I've been teaching this for a long time, so one of them shows Ben Moon on *Agincourt*, one of the world's first 8c's. How could he have been so motivated to face the effort and uncertainty? High self-efficacy, among other reasons. The principles are no different today, just the examples and grades: perhaps Adam Ondra on *La Dura Dura* (9b+). These climbers exemplify choice of behaviors (hard!), effort, persistence, learning, and achievement.

Given all these benefits, it should be obvious that we want to develop high self-efficacy, in ourselves and others. I know I certainly don't want my Stats students to have low self-efficacy. So, how does it develop? How can we promote it?

1. History: your previous successes and failures.
2. Intrinsic motivation, mastery motivation, definitions of "success."
3. Messages you hear from others.
4. Successes and failures of others: especially those who are similar to you.

Starting with number one, everyone comes to expect that the past will repeat itself—just like Lynn Hill's expectations for success. Is history controllable? You bet it is. If I choose to spend years failing on the same project to the exclusion of almost all other climbing, I will program my expectation for failure which will lead to low self-efficacy. In contrast, I could build a base of success every season and mix onsights and short-term projects (2 or 3 tries to redpoint) with my long-term projects, which will lead to high self-efficacy. The latter is likely to be more fun too. I personally enjoy onsighting and sending quickly (odd, huh?), so I seek out new warm-ups, new potential onsights, and easier projects. History is dependent on expectations—reasonable, realistic.

In *Performance Rock Climbing*, Goddard and Neumann promote the idea of a progression pyramid. The basic idea is that you shouldn't always strive to climb the next hardest grade as soon as you have done a breakthrough route. You need to have a base of experience—a few 12b's before your first 12c. I suspect the benefits here are psychological as much, or more so, than physical.

Number two, all the things that promote intrinsic motivation, mastery motivation, and definitions of "success" promote higher self-efficacy. Intrinsic: If you are doing it because it is fun and inherently rewarding, then you are more likely to choose to do it, put in more effort, and persist in the face of challenges. Mastery: If you are doing it because you want to be good for the sake of being good, rather than bragging rights, then you are more likely to reap the same benefits. Make the choice, put in the effort, and persist. Definition of success: If you view progress as success you will have more success and more fun. As a result, you will be more motivated to choose . . . effort . . . persist.

Number three, messages from others affect our beliefs about ourselves and our abilities. Explicit messages, such as "keep trying, you can do it" versus "maybe you should come down" are obvious. Implicit messages, such as smiles versus frowns and rolling eyes are less obvious, but equally influential. So, surround yourself with encouraging people. Encourage others.

Number four, our beliefs about our ability to succeed (i.e., self-efficacy) are influenced by the successes and failures of others. This is especially true when the other person is like us. Watching Sharma send 9b doesn't make me think I can send 9b (or 9a, 8c, 8b,...), but watching my weekly partner of nearly my same ability flash a 12a makes me think I have a good shot at it! A great example of this is bouldering with your regular crew. All five of you fail on a problem first go. Everyone fails, but makes progress second go. And third, fourth, fifth. But as soon as one of you tops out, the probability goes up that others will get it next go—"the send train" leaves the station. The application of point #4 is that it can be beneficial to climb with several partners of similar or slightly higher ability. You can learn from them and be motivated by them!

Summary

In this chapter, we presented many drills and exercises to help you identify and rewrite problematic scripts involving fear of failure, coping, and perfectionism. Perhaps more importantly, we offered suggestions for new—more adaptive—scripts (self-compassion, mindfulness, and self-efficacy) to replace the old ones: self-compassion, mindfulness, and self-efficacy. Use this chapter like a menu. Pick one or two items from Column A: your most problematic scripts. Then pick from Column B: effective debunking arguments. Then pick from Column C: new, better scripts. As in physical or technique training, it is best to identify one or two mental weaknesses and work on them. Don't try to change everything at once. Identify your weaknesses, those most problematic scripts. They are the ones that are holding you back in terms of performance, or spoiling your enjoyment of climbing. Focus your efforts on one or two changes and practice! Success requires repetition!

In the next chapter, we apply many of these same scripts and principles to helping others. You may find yourself helping as a partner, parent, or as a formal or informal coach. Because these applications involve formal or informal teaching and learning, we also present some of the most influential concepts from educational psychology. They have proven themselves over the years as effective guidelines for helping others to achieve success.

9 Co-Creative Coaching

By Jeff Elison and Don McGrath

❝ All coaching is, is taking a player where he can't take himself.
– *Bill McCartney, award winning football player and coach.*

In the introduction to the previous chapter, I made the point that you can use tips discussed there to help other climbers, even though the focus was on self-improvement. In this chapter our focus is on ways that partners can help each other. For the vast majority of problematic scripts, if you can identify and address them in yourself, then you can help others do the same— and vice versa.

How to Use This Chapter

As in previous chapters, your job is to identify maladaptive scripts and Beliefs. In this case, you will be identifying them in other people. And they may be identifying them in you. You can then help each other debunk scripts or help change scripts through modeling better alternatives. You may also identify problematic scripts in *your* communications with other people and expectations for other people. You can then re-script them to be more effective. Effective? Meaning more likely to help others progress or enjoy themselves. As always, success requires repetition—for you and for them.

We believe the vast majority of "coaching" in climbing is not done by formal coaches. Partners help each other. Couples help each other. Parents help their kids. Kids help their parents! Therefore, we embrace the term *co-creative coaching*, which conveys the idea that the coach isn't necessarily "superior" to the coached. In this chapter, we will describe the co-creative coaching process and provide you and your partner with tips, tools, and insights that will help you to co-creatively coach each other. In other words, we present ways to effectively assist each other with scripts involving fear of falling, fear of failure, perfectionism, and self-efficacy. We wrap up the chapter by explaining two tried-and-true principles from educational psychology that make any sort of teaching or coaching more effective.

What is Co-creative Coaching?

To co-create is to create together, alongside each other. Each party contributing what they have to offer. When you engage in co-creative coaching, you and your partner help each other improve (or have more fun). It is not a traditional coach-student relationship, but one where ideas are exchanged, experimented with, and possibly utilized to climb better.

By definition, when you engage in co-creative coaching, you and your partner voluntarily cooperate. You can't be co-creative with a partner who does not want to coach you or be coached by you. It is of utmost importance that you and your partner agree to be co-creative in order for the process to work optimally. We suggest that you share this book with your partner and ask them if they would be interested in co-creative coaching. Make sure, however, to get your book back...

Another prerequisite to effective co-creative coaching is that all participants need to have the right attitude. So, what's the right attitude? The right attitude for engaging in co-creative coaching is characterized by:

- being receptive to feedback, positive or negative
- being attentive to your partner and trying to identify things for them to consider
- being sensitive when giving feedback
- avoiding defensiveness
- avoiding being overly directive (e.g., yelling beta in the midst of your partner's attempt)

To illustrate what we mean, consider the following "coaching" exchange. In this example, Josh is struggling at a crux move while Marla is belaying and coaching him.

Josh: *Awe man, this is way hard for the grade. I just can't do this move.*

Marla: *It looks powerful.*

Josh: *Yeah, and I can't keep my butt in. OK, here goes again.* Climbing.

Marla: *Step up with your right foot. Go, go, go.*

Josh: (Slumping onto the rope). *Crap. I'm weak.*

Marla: *Are you getting tired? My neck sort of hurts.*

Josh: *OK, just let me down.*

Josh: (now on the ground) *I can't figure out what to do there.*

Marla: *I need to go pee.*

Josh: *OK*

I have to say that this is not an atypical exchange that you might hear at the crag. Let's analyze the exchange.

So, Josh is struggling and sounds frustrated. Marla's first response basically just supports that frustration yet provides no help: "It looks powerful." When Josh tries the move again, Marla kicks into beta mode and tells him what he should do. For one thing, most of us don't process verbal commands very well when we are trying a hard move. It typically distracts us.

Josh appears to get even more frustrated with himself and even verbalizes that he thinks that he is too weak to do the move. Marla follows this up by asking if he's tired and shares that she is getting tired of belaying. If Josh wasn't tired before, he is now. She offered no encouragement or perspective. When Josh gets to the ground he shares his frustration again, but Marla does not want to discuss what he could have done differently or help him address his frustration.

Now let's look at an exchange that is co-creative:

Josh: *Awe man, this is way hard for the grade. I just can't do this move.*

Marla: *Wow, you looked really good getting up to that point.*

Josh: *Yeah, but I can't keep my butt in.*

Marla: *It looks to me like your right foot is too high and holding you back from that chalked up hold out right.*

Josh: *Yeah, I feel that, but I don't see any other feet. Wait, there is this little nubbin just below the high-step. I'll try that.*

Climbing.

Josh: (slumping onto the rope again) *That felt better, but I still can't keep my butt in and it's just pulling me off.*

Marla: *Yeah, that did look better. I agree that it looks like you get scrunched up and those handholds are small. Hey, is that undercling thumb catch above you any good? It might allow you to stretch out and keep your butt in.*

Josh: *Hmmmm. Let me see. Take up. Maybe that will help hold me in while I get my foot up to the better hold. I'll try.* Climbing.

Josh pulls the move and proceeds to finish the route. Back on the ground, they continue their conversation:

Josh: *That was a very tricky crux. I don't know how I would have ever thought to do that onsight.*

Marla: *You did awesome. I did notice that when you hit that crux, you pretty quickly asked me to take you tight.*

Josh: *I didn't have any idea what to do.*

Marla: *One thing that I do sometimes when I get to a stopper move is to downclimb and see if I can get some ideas from*

a more restful spot.
Josh: *Yeah, I just didn't think about that.*
Marla: *I learned that from this great book, Vertical Mind. You should read it.*

Okay, sorry about the shameless plug. This is a very different conversation and much more productive in getting Josh to the top and in helping him learn something new. Take note of several aspects of their conversation. First, the engagement level is very high. Marla is paying attention and interested. Second, Marla suggests ideas and doesn't give commands. Third, Marla offers beta while Josh is hanging, not in the middle of moves. Fourth, Josh is open to considering what Marla has to say. Fifth, Marla sandwiches her critiques with two positive comments. This is a classic technique to help people be receptive to what they might see as negative feedback. Finally, Marla seems genuinely interested in helping Josh solve his problem.

We hope that this example gives you a sense of the attitude required for effective co-creative coaching. Attitude is extremely important, but there is more to a successful co-creative coaching relationship. A good co-creative coach can:

1. **Help set goals:** Goals are key to improving performance and accomplishing just about anything. Climbing goals can be to onsight a certain grade, to learn to lead, to redpoint a particular route, or any number of things. A coach's role in goal setting is to help their partner determine whether it's an appropriate goal or not, based on several criteria (e.g., matches partner's priorities; correct level of challenge).

   For example, suppose I climb 5.10 and I decide that I want to free the *Nose* on El Capitan. A coach might ask me how long I think it will take me to prepare and improve my climbing to where I can reach my goal. They might ask me how long I'm willing to stay motivated in reaching my goal. If I say that I want to do it within a year, they might ask me for evidence that suggests to me that that is a reasonable goal.

Likewise, if I am not pushing myself much and have an easy goal, they may ask me how excited I would be when I accomplish my goal. If I say that I'd be ecstatic, they may ask me why.

A coach can also help a climber clarify their goals. Returning to the El Cap example, a coach may ask me about my timeframe and whether the goal is to lead every pitch. They may ask whether it has to be done in one push or if I plan to fix ropes and return to the ground.

Climbers should offer their own goals, but a coach can help the climber understand whether their goal is a good one and help clarify the details.

2. **Help identify gaps in capabilities:** Another key to successful co-creative coaching is to help your partner identify gaps in capabilities required to reach the goal. If I set a goal but do not yet have all the capabilities to reach the goal, I need to work on developing them. A coach can help a climber identify the gaps and the means to address them.

Suppose that I want to redpoint *Apocalypse 91* in Rifle, a powerful and pumpy 5.13. My coach may suggest that I take a burn on it and see where I have trouble. They may suggest that my power endurance isn't where it needs to be and that I need to work on it.

Help create a plan to fill the gaps: Now the identified

gaps must be filled, so a coach can help craft a plan to address them. For me, it might be system board training in the gym, or climbing some specific routes that will build my power endurance over a period of several weeks.

3. **Help the person being coached** stay on track in their plan: An important function of a coach is to help a climber stay on track to their plan. We all get distracted and deviate from our plans. A good coach can remind us of our plan and even help to modify the plan in the event that circumstances require a change. Simple comments such as, "how's the training going?" can spark a dialog about challenges that the coach may be able to help with.

4. **Observe performance and provide feedback for improvement:** An important aspect of coaching is to provide feedback based on observations of performance. Doing this requires skill, attention and tact. The coach has to be skilled enough in climbing movement to provide meaningful suggestions. This is not to say that the coach has to be an expert climber. The best co-coaching situation is often when two climbers of fairly similar abilities coach each other.

When one is observing a climber to be coached, the coach has to pay close attention to what the climber is doing when they climb. It's easy to get distracted when belaying or spotting, but a coach has to really pay attention.

When a coach provides feedback, it needs to be given in a way that is non-judgmental, and should be as a question or suggestion, rather than a command. Instead of saying, "put your right foot in that pocket," you might say, "did you see that pocket out right?" Or you might say, "have you thought about whether that pocket might be useful?"

When providing a debriefing after a climber gets back to the ground, a coach should engage the climber in a conversation about the climb. As mentioned previously, an effective technique is to open with some positive feedback, such as, "you really looked smooth through that opening boulder problem." You then probe or make suggestions about a troublesome part of the climb. You might say, "I notice that you struggled with the fourth clip. What was going on there?"

5. **Celebrate:** A coach and climber, especially when they are co-creative coaching partners will naturally celebrate victories together. Whether it be reliving the experience around the campfire or celebrating with a favorite beverage, celebration is an important part of a co-creative coaching relationship. They are part of the reason we climb.

Coaching the *Vertical Mind* Way

As you engage in co-creative coaching with your partner, the two of you will address various aspects of climbing. Of course there are climbing technique and physical training, but those are not the central topics of this book. This book is focused on building effective scripts to defeat fear and anxiety in order to improve climbing performance and joy. The following sections provide information that will help you be a more effective coach in these areas.

Helping Others Reach Their Potential by Minimizing Fear of Falling

We've all experienced the fear of falling either in our own climbing or while belaying partners. The fear of falling is evident when we climb smoothly up to a crux, but yell "take" without really trying, or when we avoid a route that we are interested in because some of the bolts or gear appear to be far apart. These are just a few of the ways that fear of falling affects our climbing.

A coach can really help circumvent the negative effects that the fear of falling has on a climber's performance and enjoyment. There are two main ways a coach can help here: 1) Help the climber analyze a potential fall; 2) Encourage and support fall training.

In helping to analyze a potential fall, recall Ellis's ABC model and the LESSON method. You now have new tools to help your partner analyze a fall. When your partner is concerned about a particular fall, you can walk them through the LESSON checklist to see if any of the hazards exist and discuss a plan to deal with them.

You can also use Ellis's ABC model by probing your partner about what Consequence they are concerned about. You can explore the Antecedent, the conditions that lead to the consequence. Are the bolts too far apart? Is there a particular hazard to be concerned with? You can help them explore the Belief that they will fall and help them Debunk it. Is there any data to support the Belief or not? If the Beliefs are rational and the fall potentially dangerous, you can support them in their decision to skip the climb.

A coach can also help by encouraging and supporting a climber in their fall training (Chapter 6). We all need to practice falling if we are to push our climbing limits, yet most of us avoid it. Encouraging your partner to practice falling (and doing so yourself) is a great way to help minimize the fear of falling.

Helping Others Reach Their Potential by Minimizing Fear of Failure & Embarrassment

What makes a good partner? Safe, competent, skilled, re-members to bring gas money and extra beer. Sure, all of those. How about fun to be around (even on the drive and in camp), has realistic expectations for you, supportive, maybe even makes you feel good about yourself? That may seem like a lot, but it's really not that hard. Maybe you are that partner or would like to be that partner, or you find yourself formally or informally coaching other climbers. The point is that our second list of good attributes is mostly about helping other people with the fear of failure scripts we've been discussing.

In many ways, this chapter is about the flip-side, the mirror image, of the scripts described in the previous chapter. We won't repeat them all here, but as a "coach" you are now Cooley's look-ing glass. Other climbers see themselves mirrored in your eyes. They are aware that you evaluate them. Do you convey overly high expectations? Or a strict definition of success? Or the mes-sage that their worth—in your eyes—is dependent on perfor-mance? If so, you may want to re-script those. Scripts such as these have important implications for making co-creative coach-ing effective.

We're going to discuss this topic from the perspective of teaching, coaching, or even parenting, but it all still applies to being a good partner. And understanding the "giving" side of these scripts will benefit you, as well.

Recall three claims from the previous chapter: One, the Be-lief that approval/love/acceptance/self-worth depend on perfor-mance may be the most important irrational Belief on Ellis's list. Two, we claimed it underlies many other maladaptive scripts and irrational Beliefs. Three, we said it is easy to learn this Belief be-cause parents, siblings, friends, partners, teachers, and coaches praise us when we do well and may not (or worse) when we do poorly. Hopefully you already see where this is going—don't do that to other people.

There are many ways we can accidentally convey the message that the degree to which we value other people depends on how well they do. Simple smiles, congratulations, and displays of pride in others can backfire IF we don't show acceptance and support in response to lesser performances. Parents are often advised to respond as follows when their kid does wrong: "You're not a bad kid, you just did a bad thing." The idea is to acknowledge their mistake, while conveying love or acceptance. We can convey a similar message when we give feedback. In fact, doing so *makes* the feedback more constructive.

Psychologists describe this message as **unconditional positive regard**. Hard to achieve, but what a wonderful ideal—I accept you in spite of your flaws, quirks, and mistakes. Most of us would like unconditional positive regard from partners, coaches, teachers, parents, and especially significant others. We wouldn't have to hide anything about ourselves. We could just be ourselves, without shame or embarrassment. Nice ideal.

We can approach this ideal another way and specifically address other scripts by conveying *our* definition of success. When my partner attempts a redpoint and makes it one move higher, I can acknowledge that as progress—a success. I can even explicitly recognize the progress: "You looked much more solid on the third clip and you made it a move higher." That really conveys progress, maybe solidifies it in his mind, and it shows that I'm not so self-centered that I don't pay attention to his climbing and his progress.

Conveying the definition of success as progress also promotes some of the good stuff we discussed in Chapter 3: intrinsic motivation (this is fun) over extrinsic motivation (I'm doing this for others); and mastery orientation (I want to improve) over performance orientation (ultimate success is all that matters).

Being this kind of partner promotes **self-efficacy**, the extremely important psychological concept discussed in the previous chapter. In summary, unconditional positive regard and recognizing progress move you up on our list: fun to be around, realistic expectations, supportive, making others feel good about themselves.

Messages about expectations can be broadcast in additional ways that affect our partners. Imagine teaching something that many people find difficult, say Statistics, one of my favorite courses to teach. Students fear it, so you have a real opportunity to help them overcome their fears. Why do they fear it? For the same reasons climbers fear climbing: failure, embarrassment, looking incompetent. Therefore, if you are successful in addressing those fears and guiding them to progress, they recognize and appreciate it. Being a competent teacher/coach is a first step. That means not only knowing statistics/climbing yourself, but knowing how to get new information across in a way that students can successfully learn. These are separate abilities. It's that second ability that we are discussing here because a big part of it is helping them past their fears.

Our messages about expectations matter. Realistic is best. It's so tempting to tell a statistics student or a partner: "It's easy, no problem." We *think* we are being encouraging. But that backfires when it isn't easy *for them*. You just conveyed the fact that it is easy *for you*, so: One, you must be better than them; and Two, they are falling short of your expectations, so there must be something wrong with them. It is much better to say: "This is a hard concept (or move), but you can get it. You may make mistakes, they are natural and expected, but you will learn from them." Saying that conveys realistic expectations—both for you and them.

You even need to be careful with realistic expectations. A regular partner of mine (so I know her abilities well) admitted that she feels more pressure when we yell, "You've got it!" We think we are just being encouraging, but in her mind, we just yelled our expectations for her performance!

A final problem arises directly from our competence—we don't make mistakes (or few) —when we are helping the less experienced with easier climbs or undergraduate statistics. They see us performing flawlessly and it doesn't occur to them that we once struggled with the same things they are. You can take two approaches here. First, flat-out tell them you had a hard time when you were there. Even with 35-plus years of climbing behind me, I love having a partner tell me: "I really struggled with that deadpoint before I could send." Second, look for opportunities to make mistakes, or call attention to your real mistakes.

A good friend of mine is a ski instructor who designed a program specifically for older beginners. He knew their biggest challenge was fear of embarrassment. They were afraid to fall, afraid to act like "kids," afraid to make mistakes. These fears were holding them back or completely preventing them from skiing. Sound familiar? It did to me too, so we have discussed these commonalities around the campfire for hours. In his program, he would intentionally look for opportunities to fall over to show that crashing happens to the best of us. Since he started the ski program for beginners indoors, he would get down on the floor and roll around with them to reacquaint them with the feel of play—play that had become unnatural for them—and to break through their fears of embarrassment.

Improve Coping

Just as we can improve our own Compass of Shame coping styles, we can help others when it comes to coping. First, we can recognize these styles as problematic, and if appropriate, explain what is going on. For example, the fourth-grader who beats up every kid who threatens his ego is using Attack Other. It may be protecting his ego in the short-term, but the long-term consequences will be worse when he finds himself friendless or worse. Second, we can model graceful coping ourselves. *Modeling* in psychology means one person does something (models the behavior) and someone else imitates it. Like media violence. But it can be positive behavior too. "Wow, look at how cool she was about falling off her project. She's still having a good time and smiling." Opportunities to model adaptive coping are especially likely to occur in a co-creative coaching arrangement, since you and your partner may have similar abilities and face challenges and failures at a similar rate.

Perfectionism

As with coping, you can model good or bad perfectionism for others. Part of this modeling *is* graceful coping, rather than Attack Self rumination. Part of it is saying, "oh well," and trying again. And a big part of it is sharing your expectations and definition of success—which should not mean flawless.

When my daughter was around two or three, her mother and I noticed what looked like early indicators of perfectionism. For example, she would have a meltdown over major tragedies like coloring outside the lines in her coloring book. As I mentioned in the previous chapter, I have some personal and family history with the downside of perfectionism. In fact, my own tendencies may have served as a model for my daughter. (She would often see me throw my crayons…) I didn't want to see her become another unhappy perfectionist. So, her mother and I devised a plan that included intentional mistakes, followed by adaptive coping—the "oh well" and trying again mentioned previously.

It worked—quickly! Because she hadn't had years of beating down the neural paths underlying those perfectionism scripts, she responded in just a few months. And now I'm proud to say she is a drug-addicted beauty-school dropout…no, no, no, I'm proud of her for being such a well-adjusted, motivated person.

Not all of my climbing and parenting stories are successes, but the failures often illustrate important points as well. Case in point—counting attempts. At one point, I was informally coaching two friends who were relatively new to climbing. Both had talent and were progressing rapidly. Being the stats/numbers guy that I am, I have always kept a climbing log and always counted my attempts on redpoints. I started doing the same for them in order to make their progress clear. It worked for a while—when progress was constant. However, years later we all had a conversation in which they described the de-motivating effects for them. Counting attempts had become habitual and when they weren't in top shape, it just depressed them. It turned out that this wasn't very effective co-creative coaching. Other climbers and trainers have noted this perfectionistic problem and suggested better scripts. For example, count attempts up to three; after that just lump all redpoints together.

If counting attempts motivates you, then it's not a problematic script. If it de-motivates you, then change that script!

Self-Efficacy

We discussed the many benefits of high *self-efficacy* in the previous chapter. Effective coaching can help others raise their self-efficacy. Effective co-creative coaching can raise both partners self-efficacy.

To promote it in others, let's revisit how it develops:

- History: *Their* previous successes and failures
- *Their* intrinsic motivation, mastery motivation, definitions of "success"
- Messages *they* hear (or see) from others
- Successes and failures of others—especially those who are similar to *them*

First, just as we have control to shape our own history, we may be able to help others shape their histories. History is dependent on expectations—reasonable, realistic. Encouraging someone to get on climbs that are too hard for them will diminish self-efficacy. But so will showing a lack of confidence in them. This is apparent in our discussion of co-creative coaching.

Number two, we can promote intrinsic motivation by making climbing fun. Don't make it feel like work. We can promote mastery motivation by focusing on other climbers' learning and progress, rather than their tick-lists. We can promote broader definitions of "success."

Number three, your verbal and non-verbal messages affect other climbers' beliefs about themselves and their abilities.

Number four, their beliefs about their ability to succeed are influenced by the successes and failures of others. Most strongly by others who are like them. This is good news if we are talking about co-creative coaching among climbers of similar abilities. If, however, you are a much stronger climber, you may actually slow a less-experienced climber's progress by always picking the climbs, taking the lead, or putting up a top-rope. It can be very beneficial to have less-experienced climbers spend some time climbing with others like themselves. It can be comforting for them to see each other struggle *and* motivating to see each other succeed.

Self-Efficacy in Action

Quite a few years ago I was a participant in a series of inter-actions that has become my prototypical example for the princi-ples of self-efficacy. I signed up for a community service program much like Big Brothers. I was matched with Ben, a 13-year-old boy who was thought by the directors and his mother to be at considerable risk. Ben's grades were very low and he often missed school. Art was the only subject where he excelled. Math was his nemesis. He was convinced he was stupid.

I was looking forward to getting to know Ben and helping him in whatever way I could. I had the common sense to make our first meeting light-hearted and fun. And then I jumped head-first into a ridiculous mistake during our second meeting. Being a math and science guy, I was sure I could help clear up all his confusions about math. I asked if I could help him with his homework. He immediately made mistakes, became over-whelmingly embarrassed, and shut down. He wasn't the dumb one; I was. Here was a young boy who just wanted a new friend, someone to accept him, and I had just asked him to share with me something he wanted to hide—something about which he was deeply ashamed. Ben had a long, long history of failures with math. These failures had become scripted: "I can't do math, I'm no good at it, I'm stupid, I should just give up." And we played out that script on the spot. He gave up and I couldn't get him to open the book. I couldn't reassure him that it was okay. Ben had very low self-efficacy when it came to math. It affected his choices, his effort, his persistence, and his learning.

So now the other side of the story.... Ben knew I was a rock climber and wanted to try it. This time I had sense enough to start him on easier climbs and set him up for success. That was good, but my friends and I accidently did something much, much better—without even realizing what we were doing. We included him in our bouldering sessions. At that time, I had a small climbing wall in my basement. My climbing partners would come over to train together. A snapshot of a typical bouldering session would include three or four of us taking turns on some new boulder problem. One of us would try it and fall, and then the next guy would fall, and then the next gal would fall . . . and we would start all over again. Success wasn't gauged by reaching the top. Encouragement did not depend on reaching the top. Encouragement poured out in shouts whenever anyone tried extra hard or reached one hold higher than before. One of us would get a foot higher, fall off, and be greeted with slaps on the back, smiles, and high fives. At the time, I had no idea that we were teaching Ben an important lesson.

After a few weeks of these training sessions, my partners and I noticed Ben's rapid progress, his joy and excitement for climbing. Most importantly, we noticed that he wasn't bothered by falling—his "mistakes" and "failures." Why? Because, without preaching or explicitly teaching, we had implicitly conveyed a whole host of messages, a whole set of scripts. Trying is what matters. *Progress* equals success. We don't judge each other for our mistakes; we learn from them. We are willing to risk making mistakes because that is the *only* way we will improve. It is SAFE to push yourself and make mistakes with us. I'm sure that last message was one Ben had not learned regarding math. He developed high self-efficacy for climbing.

Closing Comments on Self-Efficacy

Two closing notes on self-efficacy will be helpful. First, "high" self-efficacy is good, but it should be fairly realistic. What if Ondra's self-efficacy had been so high that he went to redpoint *Change* and decided instead to leave the rope behind and solo it? Point being, too high can lead to dangerous choices.

Second, we want to develop **resilient** self-efficacy. Self-efficacy is scripted, it is learned. Learning theory has revealed that the principles of learning are similar in pigeons, rats, and humans. You learn fastest when the outcome is consistent (e.g., always succeed or always get the food pellet). Implication? Create lots of success for you or the other person initially (start of career or start of season). BUT, consistent outcomes have a downside—we notice immediately when the outcome changes: "Hey, no food pellet" or "Wait a minute, I fell." This can rattle expectations and we can unlearn them (and self-efficacy) quickly. Therefore, maximally effective coaching and teaching should intersperse failures.

The ideal pattern is lots of successes early in the learning phase, followed by a failure, more successes, a failure, successes…. Over time, failures can become more frequent and beneficial because this pattern builds **resilience**! In other words, we aren't devastated by a failure. It doesn't destroy self-efficacy or change our expectations. Self-efficacy becomes more solid and it gets easier to persevere in the face of difficulties.

To optimize the mix of successes and failures you need to pay careful attention to the emotional reactions and motivations of the learner. Are they getting discouraged or angry? Giving up more quickly? Or enjoying themselves in spite of "failures"? Persevering longer and longer?

That's just what I want in my students—perseverance and effort in the face of difficult Statistics. And that's just what leads to the achievements of climbers like Lynn Hill, Ben Moon, Chris Sharma, and Adam Ondra.

Scaffolding and the Zone of Proximal Development

Now, let's turn to two extremely effective principles of teaching. A Russian educational psychologist named Lev Vygotsky described two principles that forever changed my approach to coaching, teaching, and parenting: *scaffolding* and the *Zone of Proximal Development* (ZPD). Most of us have thought about these concepts and perhaps do them instinctively to some extent. However, Vygotsky's elaborate descriptions spell them out, making them easier to apply.

All of us have seen scaffolding around a building, the temporary structure that allows workers access during construction. In Vygotsky's case, scaffolding is a metaphor for the many ways in which we assist other people while they are learning something new. We help them build their skills and knowledge. In climbing, we scaffold with beta, encouragement, training tips, technique demonstrations, taking weight off during spotting, and even tips on belaying and clipping. Scaffolding can be a double-edged sword—too little or too much can slow progress. That fact leads directly to the concept of the ZPD—the zone where optimal coaching/learning occurs.

The zone lies between two boundaries (Figure 9.1; left side of cylinder). At the "easy" end, the lower boundary is the Independent Level—what a learner can do on their own, without help. At the upper end, the boundary is the Assisted Level—the

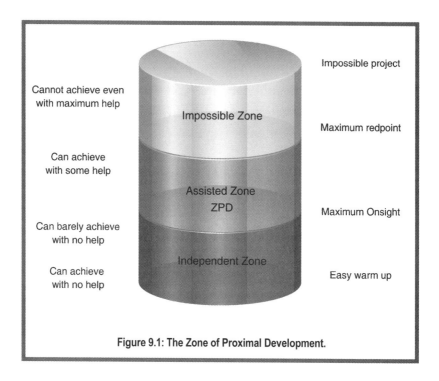

Figure 9.1: The Zone of Proximal Development.

maximum a learner can do with assistance (i.e., scaffolding). The ZPD consists of all the challenges between these two levels. This is where maximal learning occurs.

Putting the ZPD in climbing terms (Figure 9.1; right side of cylinder), Vygotsky would define it as all the climbing challenges that fall between two levels. At the easy end are all the routes or boulder problems you can do on your own, with no falls or beta. At the top end are the routes or problems you could top out with tons of help: beta, tension, falls. Learning and progress will be most rapid in-between these two levels, the ZPD.

In our discussion of self-efficacy, we mentioned that it can be counter-productive to encourage other climbers to get on climbs that are too hard for them. Vygotsky would have said the same thing, for some different reasons. While climbs that are too hard will erode self-efficacy, Vygotsky would add they also lead to frustration and slow learning. Imagine the tradeoff: hang on the end of the rope for hours unable to link two moves while your belayer pulls you up or spend the same time and effort completing a few routes that require beta and a fall or two. The latter would clearly be a better investment of time, energy, and skin.

Similarly, having too little confidence in someone you are coaching, discouraging them from pushing into the ZPD, is counter-productive. They won't feel challenged, and as a result, may feel de-motivated. Progress will slow and they may even suffer from boredom. Most experienced climbers embrace the advice that you must push yourself to falling in order to progress optimally.

Too hard → frustration, de-motivation, lower self-efficacy, less learning, slower progress

Too easy → little challenge, boredom, de-motivation, less learning, slower progress

When we are in the position of teacher, parent, or coach we should:

1. Assess the learner's ZPD, their Independent Level and Assisted Level—formally or informally.
2. Tailor tasks (e.g., climbs) to be appropriate for this ZPD.
3. Apply the appropriate level of scaffolding. Not too much, not too little.

Let's look at some concrete examples of Do's and Don'ts:

1. Assess ZPD: This can be easy in climbing due to well-es-

tablished grading systems. Independent Level = "She can flash 10a, struggles on 10b, falls on 10c." Assisted Level = "She can redpoint 11c with a great deal of time and help, but 11d seems impossible for her."

    a. Do: Of course strengths and weaknesses in particular styles (e.g., slabs vs. overhangs) will complicate assessment. So, refine assessment across a variety of styles: "She falls on 10b slabs, but doesn't fall until 10d on overhangs." "He climbs harder grades on plastic than rock."

    b. Do: Pay attention to the learner's climbing, so you can judge his ZPD accurately. This is one reason why (very) small classrooms and individualized coaching are more effective than their alternatives.

    c. Do: Take into account specifics of the day: fatigue, distractions, emotional states.

    d. Don't: Assume their ZPD will stay static from day-to-day or across techniques.

2. Tailor tasks by picking climbs, boulder problems, drills, or exercises of the "right" difficulty.

    a. Do: In a given day or session, walk them through a sequence of warm ups, mild challenges, serious challenges. At each point in the sequence, you need to keep in mind their ZPD—for example, what is mildly challenging for them. The ZPD is especially critical when picking the "serious challenges" because these have the greatest potential to illicit gains if chosen properly, or de-motivation if they are too hard.

    b. Do: Keep this climber's motivation, frustration tolerance, fear of failure, and injury proneness in mind. If the learner is motivated, then you want to push them toward the top end of their ZPD.

c. Do: Related to 2.b, consider this climber's self-efficacy. If it's just forming, then target the lower end of their ZPD to increase the probability of success and build self-efficacy. If the climber has resilient, relatively high self-efficacy, then they should show greater persistence and handle greater challenges.

d. Do: Finally, target weaknesses if the learner has sufficient self-efficacy to face their weaknesses. We all stand to make the greatest gains when we train our weaknesses as opposed to the areas where we are already strong. We agree 100% with other authors who emphasize this point (e.g., Goddard & Neumann; MacLeod).

e. Don't: Fail to challenge the learner by picking climbs that are too easy. Perhaps an even more common mistake is repeating the same climbs over and over. There is something to be learned from repeating climbs in better style by correcting mistakes, but there is a point of diminishing returns.

f. Don't: Conversely, don't waste valuable energy, skin, and training time by throwing them on impossible projects.

3. Provide the "appropriate" level of scaffolding. This goal requires great creativity.

a. Do: Make them *work*! Neuroscience clearly shows that improvements in memory and scripts (i.e., stronger neural connections) are gained during the retrieval/ execution phase.

i. While weight training, you won't get stronger as quickly if your spotter grabs the bar too soon or assists you too much. Your greatest gains come from those few seconds when you struggle maximally.

ii. While studying, you won't improve memory as quickly if someone gives you the full answer. You will improve more if you struggle to recall the answer with minimal help/scaffolding.

iii. Similarly in climbing, the climber has to do the work—struggle to make the move physically, figure it out mentally, or execute the correct script.

b. Do: 3.a means you should provide the minimal scaffolding necessary to help the learner progress. This is where the creativity comes in. What tiny hint, bit of help, or advice will move them forward *while making them work to do the rest*?

c. Do: Explain the whys. Providing beta may be the best option—in the moment—but explain why it works when they come down. The "whys" are the general principles that will allow them to generalize from this specific move to all similar moves in the future. Why do you flag? How do you recognize when to flag?

d. Do: Building on 3.c, train technique systematically. Identify a weakness—they don't flag. Pick a boulder problem or short route where they should flag. Demonstrate it. Explain what it feels like when you recognize the need to flag. Explain the physics of why it works. Let them practice it so they get both the feel of needing to flag and the feel of when it works.

e. Don't: Automatically spray them with running beta. You are robbing them of opportunities to learn.

f. Don't: Automatically give them tension or take their weight.

g. Don't: Spoil their onsights.

Let me illustrate these principles using another domain right out of educational psychology. When my daughter was young, we read together almost every night. As I said previously, Vygotsky changed my whole approach. Before understanding the ZPD and scaffolding, I made many mistakes. For example, I chose to read *The Hobbit* before she was ready. We spent months slogging through a book when she could have been reading more productive, appropriate-level books. We were both unnecessarily frustrated. I slowed her reading progress. I had chosen a 5.8 book when she was a 5.4 reader.

As soon as she struggled to read a word, I blurted it out. I robbed her of opportunities to strengthen those neural pathways and practice sounding out words. Again, I slowed her progress. It was like shouting out the next move on a climb before she had a chance to try it on her own.

After I learned about the ZPD and scaffolding, reading was much more productive. We chose books with more appropriate levels of difficulty. I scaffolded patiently, with minimal help, reminding her of general principles. For example, when she struggled, I would sound-out one or two letters instead of the whole word or remind her of the sound of similar words. When she mispronounced words, I reminded her of general rules, such as when "e" is silent.

It was all a great success—she is now a 21-year-old who reads at a fifth-grade level and redpoints 5.6. (Not really.)

Optimal scaffolding really does require great creativity and attention. That's why it is so much easier with small classes or individual coaching, just like assessing the ZPD. The ability to tailor scaffolding well is one of the most important attributes that makes a good teacher or coach.

Summary

Hopefully, our descriptions of co-creative coaching, self-efficacy, the ZPD, and scaffolding have given you helpful ideas. We firmly believe these are effective principles to optimize your climbing experiences and those of your partners. Everyone should be able to improve performance and make climbing more enjoyable, if that's what they desire.

Optimal experience is what we are after and it is a pseudonym for "flow," the topic of our next chapter. Co-creative coaching can increase the frequency of those rewarding moments of flow.

10 Flow–Putting It All Together, Performance and Play

By Jeff Elison

❝ I'm really trying to incorporate a much more intuitive flow
and trust in my body. It's a really tough line between using
your calculating mind and your intuitive side, but the most
beautiful climbing is when both of those come together.

– Lynn Hill

Flow Characterized ("In the Zone, Dude!")

Unless you have lived a very impoverished life, you have found yourself "in the zone" or "on the ball" or "in the groove" or "wired in" or "with your head in the game." All these phrases are examples of flow. Flow is defined as the mental state of operation in which a person in an activity is fully immersed in a feeling of energized focus, full involvement, and success in the process of the activity. In the seminal work on the topic, the creator of the flow theory, Csíkszentmihályi, describes flow as "the state in which people are so involved in an activity that nothing else seems to matter; the experience itself is so enjoyable that people will do it even at great cost, for the sheer sake of doing it." Flow is when you get to the anchors and say: "Wow, I can't believe I just pulled that off; everything just clicked."

Take a minute and try to remember a time or times when you experienced flow. They may be examples from climbing or from other activities. Narrow it down to one prime example before reading on.

Write a brief description here:
_____
_____
_____
_____

I mentioned the "impoverished life" because these moments of flow are intensely rewarding. If heroin addicts chase the tiger, then a lot of climbers chase flow. We want it again. We placed this chapter near the end of the book because flow is where it all comes together: "it" meaning performance and "fun"—or at least intensely positive experience. Flow is also where it all comes together in another way: physical and mental training—Vertical Mind! But just what is flow?

Most of us recognize flow when it happens; however, we may not consciously recognize all of its components. Ten main components of flow have been identified. The following list describes them to assist you in recognizing them. See how well they describe that experience I asked you to remember.

1. **Clear goals** (rules, expectations). For example, onsighting and redpointing are pretty clearly defined.
2. **Concentration is required.** Concentration limits our attention to the task at hand.
3. **Loss of self-consciousness/self-awareness/ego.** This has also been described as the merging of action and awareness. We no longer evaluate how we look to others or what our performance indicates about us. Evaluations are focused on what to do next.
4. **Distorted sense of time** (slower or faster). "It seemed like I left the ground and the next thing I knew I was clipping the chains." Or, "I was too pumped to clip, so I skipped the bolt and punched it to the anchor. It all happened in slow motion."
5. **Direct and immediate feedback** . . . allows us to tune our behavior. This one is usually clear in climbing: getting pumped, slipping, grabbing the right or wrong hold—in the right or wrong way.
6. **Sense of personal control.** Gives us a sense of ownership. If you send, it's all you, which promotes flow. In contrast, a rollercoaster ride may be exciting and have some of these other features, but is unlikely to lead to flow.
7. **Activity is intrinsically rewarding.** Outcomes may matter, but we love climbing for many other reasons, such as the immediate feel of moving over rock. Climbing may feel "effortless," even when we know what we just did was hard.

8. **Lack of awareness of bodily needs.** We may be so engaged that we forget about hunger or thirst.
9. **Absorption in the activity.** Nothing else exists when you are flowing on a route.
10. **Balance between challenge and skill.** Flow tasks require skill/competence. Balance means you have what is needed to match the demands of the current challenge.

Sound familiar? I'm guessing that at least five or six of these were apparent in your personal example of flow. Description is nice, but how can you use this information? As it turns out, some of these ten characteristics are features of the experience, while three are controllable conditions that promote flow.

Flow Predictors:

Facilitating Flow Experiences (for Self & Others)

Knowing the conditions that promote flow allows us to chase the experience with greater success. It also suggests pointers for helping other people achieve flow. The three controllable conditions that promote flow are clear goals, feedback, and balance between challenge and skill. As I said previously, the first two conditions are usually pretty obvious in climbing. However, you may want to define goals other than onsighting or redpointing, depending on the situation. Smoothly linking a section of your project or executing a technique drill could be appropriate goals. Setting sub-goals may be especially important for beginning climbers to encourage focus, feelings of success, enjoyment, and flow.

In-the-moment, external feedback is difficult to incorporate during a flow experience. It is counter to other aspects of flow, such as focused attention and loss of self-consciousness. However, good feedback from our partners can facilitate progress toward higher levels of performance. It should be clear that this point overlaps with Don's discussion of co-creative coaching partnerships. Anything that improves performance can increase flow, because performance is integral to the third condition—balance. Balance is the variable over which you have the most control.

Balance between challenge and skill/ability means you have some chance of success, but success is not a sure thing. To promote flow, the level of challenge should be somewhere between demanding-enough-to-hold-your-attention and really-pushing-your-limits. Theory tells us that a 5.14 climber is unlikely to experience flow on a 5.7, and a 5.7 climber just isn't going to experience flow on a 5.14. The flow diagram (Figure 10.1) illustrates the complex relationships between challenge and skill. The 5.7 climber would find himself in the upper-left corner while on a 5.14—anxious, terrified, or unable to make any moves. The 5.14 climber would find herself in the lower-right corner—relaxed, possibly bored, possibly having fun—while on a 5.7.

I certainly do not mean to imply that climbing easy (for you) routes is a bad thing. I find it very fun and enjoyable. Some of my best days have been spent cruising up classics with good friends, great weather, and great scenery. My point is simply that you are less likely to experience optimal performance and flow when the level of challenge is low. However, Helen Hooper studied flow for her master's thesis, specifically among rock climbers, and found that many climbers still reported flow while on climbs that were easy, relative to their abilities.

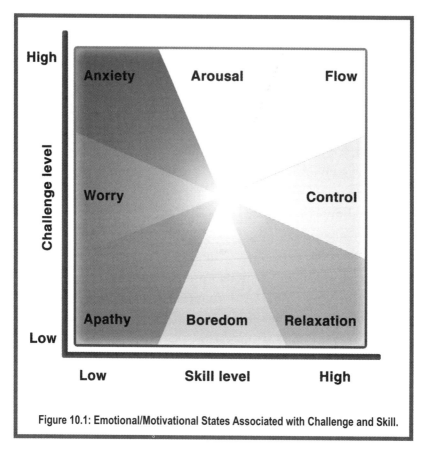

Figure 10.1: Emotional/Motivational States Associated with Challenge and Skill.

Figure 10.1 is based on research which shows that balance is not enough. The low-skill, low-challenge combination is likely to lead to apathy. This describes some of my students who don't even know why they are in college. The point is that, to promote flow, you need balance and moderate-to-high levels of challenge/skill. This combination of factors is sometimes referred to as the flow channel because of the narrow set of conditions involved. Bad news for beginners, but this fact offers one more reason to keep climbing. Once again, Hooper's thesis demonstrates that flow may be more widespread in climbing than theory would lead us to expect. She found that climbers of all levels reported flow. Nevertheless, skill and competence are rewarding, including greater frequency of flow experiences!

Maintaining the balance between challenge and skill can be tricky, but the balance is controllable to varying degrees. Controlling the balance may be easier in sports like mountain biking, snowboarding, and skiing where speed and choice of line can often be modified very quickly. "Should I brake or not?" "Should I take the narrow line through the trees or the open slope?"

However, there are several choices available in climbing that affect this balance, in addition to the choice of route:

- Rests: Take the rest or keep moving to make it harder.
- Line: You can choose the line in terms of traversing to a rest, going directly over the bulge, straight over the bolts, etc.
- Beta: Choose easier or harder beta. If you are repeating a route, you may force yourself to do it a different way.
- Handicap: Running shoes, barefoot, no chalk, no rope, etc. Or if you are a horribly bored Rifle climber, try high-heels and tutu (Steve Landin on Pump-O-Rama, 5.13a) or naked with a watermelon dangling from your harness (Charley Bentley on Vitamin H, 5.12+).
- Speed: Climbing faster than your normal pace can be conducive to flow for multiple reasons. It increases the challenge, but also forces you to climb intuitively and make decisions more quickly. In addition, the pace makes it harder to think self-consciously and it increases your momentum. I often find myself making bigger moves, skipping holds, and discovering new sequences.

The challenge-skill balance is fragile, even with these tips. As a result, you may find yourself experiencing flow for just one part of a route, often referred to as "micro-flow." Relish those moments. They are better than nothing, much better.

It can be reassuring when psychological principles from different theorists converge. Notice what happens when you step outside the flow channel. Too much challenge leads to worry, anxiety, and frustration, just like stepping beyond the Zone of Proximal Development, discussed in the previous chapter. Conversely, too little challenge leads to apathy and boredom, again paralleling Vygotsky's points about the ZPD. And both theories point out the effects on performance and learning when you step outside these boundaries. Neither performance nor learning is optimal when you step outside the flow channel or ZPD.

Climbing Is Conducive to Flow

Hooper's thesis seems to imply that flow experiences may be more common among rock climbers than among participants in many other sports. Every climber in her study reported having experienced flow! Beginners reported flow more frequently than we would expect based on theory. Experienced climbers reported flow under conditions that theory would not predict: on easy routes. Perhaps the prevalence of flow in rock climbing is precisely because climbing integrates so many factors that promote flow. The challenges of climbing, the mental puzzles, demand our attention. Similarly, fear may help sharpen our focus. Hooper thought this last point was especially true for beginners. In addition, the ease with which challenge can be matched to ability allows us to find the flow channel.

My personal experiences fit nicely with flow theory and Hooper's data. Climbing, even on easier routes or boulder problems I have wired, can rapidly induce a meditative state. My favorite example is bouldering after a hard day at work. I can't count the times that I left work stressed, with my head swimming, hardly able to focus. I'd walk the short distance to the boulders of Horsetooth Reservoir, pull on my shoes, chalk up, and ten minutes later the bad day was erased from my mind. The stress was gone. My attention was completely directed to the task at hand: movement, challenges, and fun.

Attention, Working Memory, and Mindfulness

There are other important parallels between flow and psychological concepts we have already encountered. Recall that working memory (e.g., short-term memory), consciousness, and attention are limited resources. We can only think about so much at one time. This limitation has its pros and cons. On the downside, it limits performance. On the upside, it accounts for some of the uniqueness of the flow state. Because working memory and attention are maxed out by the demands of the challenge, we experience complete focus. Our working memories have no room for concerns about self-evaluation or evaluation by others (e.g., how do I look?), so we lose self-consciousness. We also lose track of time and bodily needs. We are completely absorbed (Figure 10.2).

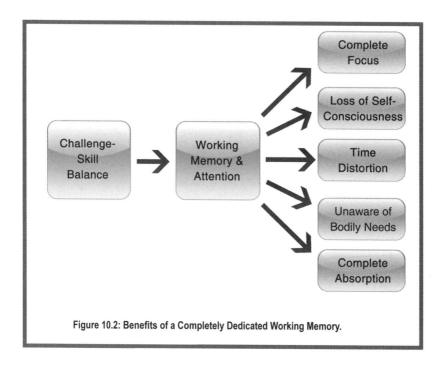

Figure 10.2: Benefits of a Completely Dedicated Working Memory.

Figure 10.2 also illustrates why some of the suggestions from previous chapters influence performance and flow. For example, fear of failure is largely about concern over other people's evaluations of us. If fear of failure is high, then loss of self-consciousness is unlikely to occur because our concerns intrude on working memory—the arrow reverses direction. Flow and performance are impeded. So, reducing fear of failure promotes flow and performance. Similarly, bodily concerns like hunger, fatigue, pain, and too much fear of falling intrude on working memory. Again, the arrow reverses direction. These dynamics make it clear why mindfulness is beneficial. When thoughts intrude, we train ourselves to let them pass. As usual, scripting mindfulness requires practice. But, that practice will likely pay off in increased performance and more flow experiences.

Finally, our old friend automaticity from Chapter 2 plays a significant role in flow. Recall that automaticity arises from over-learning. After much practice, thoughts and movements emerge reliably, smoothly, without conscious effort. We climb intuitively. This is the definition of skill. Automaticity explains why flow is more likely to occur at the top right corner of Figure 10.1, where challenge and skill are both high. Although challenge and skill are balanced at the bottom left corner, balance isn't enough—you need skill and automaticity for thought and movement to flow.

In Chapter 2, I made the point that automaticity frees up consciousness for more important decision making. Flow promotes a perfect union of automaticity and concentrated attention, uninhibited by ego. Lynn Hill's quote in the epigraph captures these dynamics of flow perfectly. Flow requires the intuitive side and the calculating mind. And "the most beautiful climbing is when both of those come together."

Flow and Learning

When I pointed out the commonalities between flow and the zone of proximal development, I alluded to the positive effects on learning as another parallel. Csíkszentmihályi explicitly mentions enhanced learning as one of the benefits of flow. When in a flow state, you are completely focused. Attention and working memory are dedicated to the task at hand. You are intrinsically motivated because you enjoy what you are doing. These are ideal conditions for learning—in the moment. However, they are also ideal in the long-term. You want to repeat the experience for its own sake. Moreover, you don't just repeat the same climb, you up the ante to maintain the challenge-skill balance and maintain interest. So, flow has long-term effects on learning. You may feel like you are learning without trying because you are climbing for the sake of climbing. It doesn't feel like "exercise" or "training."

In his book, *50 Athletes Over 50*, Don noted how important all of this is to maintaining exercise, athletics, and health over the long-term.

The Autotelic Personality

Although we cannot force ourselves to enter flow or predict when we will enter flow, we have discussed a list of variables that affect flow and that are under our control to some degree. Csíkszentmihályi describes a final set of variables as the autotelic personality. "Auto" refers to self and "telic" to goals.

This personality type is exemplified by a person who is:

- curious, interested
- goal-directed
- enjoys life
- does things for their own sake
- internally motivated (e.g., joy, learning, achievement), rather than by external goals (e.g., fame, money)
- persistent

Genetics plays some role in the autotelic personality. As we have seen, anxiety, fear, fear of failure, and high self-consciousness are detrimental to flow and performance. All of these are influenced by genetics. However, the characteristics of the autotelic personality are also learned, scripted. In fact, many are learned during childhood. They may be promoted by autotelic families. They may be promoted by positive experiences in school or sports at a young age, especially when school or sports include interesting challenges and appropriate levels of support. In contrast, too much pressure, unrealistic challenges, and criticism may spoil learning and sporting experiences and self-efficacy, leading to something short of the autotelic personality. Scripts involving fear and avoidance of challenges and public situations may develop instead. Instead of being goal-directed, persistent, and intrinsically motivated, we may become scripted to shy away from challenges, give up easily, and derive little pleasure from overcoming challenges. You may be able to see these influences (e.g., an autotelic family) at work in your own development.

Putting It All Together

As with other positive outcomes I have discussed, we have some control to promote flow in ourselves and others. We can shape individual situations to improve the probability of experiencing flow. We can develop characteristics of the autotelic personality or model them for others.

> Exercise 1: Sketch your ideal circumstances for achieving your own flow state, based on the controllable factors I discussed (e.g., difficulty of climb to achieve challenge-skill balance, type of climbing, clear goals, pace).
>
> _____
> _____
> _____
> _____

> Exercise 2: If you are in a "coaching" role with someone else, write a sketch of how you might help them structure ideal circumstances to promote their experiences of flow.
>
> _____
> _____
> _____
> _____

Flow is worth these efforts. As Csíkszentmihályi writes, "a good life is one that is characterized by complete absorption in what one does." That complete absorption produces the enjoyment and high levels of performance we desire. In those flow experiences, we think more clearly, we play with purpose, and we send with optimal performances. In the next chapter, we integrate the psychological concepts from previous chapters into the *Vertical Mind* framework, which we call **Think-Play-Send**, to offer additional exercises and drills to improve performance, increase enjoyment, and promote flow.

Getting Started

By Don McGrath

> **Action is the foundational key to all success.**
> – Pablo Picasso

In the preceding chapters, you've learned about the nature of fear and how it affects climbing performance. You've seen how it is a double-edged sword, one that can motivate you or shut you down. You've also learned about how we learn through play, repeatedly experimenting in a safe environment, which builds "paths in the snow" that allow us to move tasks from conscious memory to automatic responses. Once these paths are established, we harden them by practicing in emotion-filled situations—at speed and in the moment. Exercising these automata enables us to draw upon them when we need them in difficult situations—when thinking is not possible or very difficult.

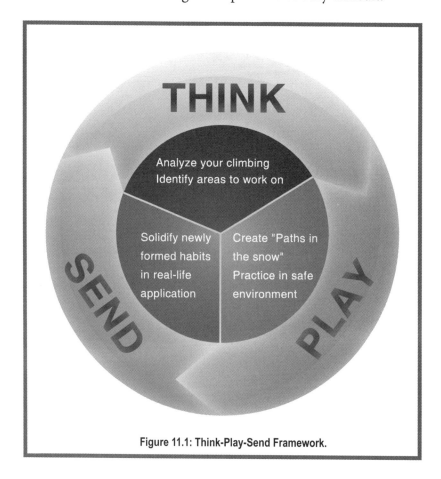

Figure 11.1: Think-Play-Send Framework.

In this chapter, we outline the Think-Play-Send process (Figure 11.1), which allows you to systematically identify roadblocks that stunt your climbing, and we help you overcome them. In practice, select one or two aspects of your climbing to improve upon and target these with exercises that create habits that improve performance. You can apply this process repeatedly, focusing on new aspects of your climbing each time.

The chapter is organized into three sections: Think, Play, Send—each presenting integrated mind-body exercises. If you implement the exercises and processes outlined in this chapter, your rock climbing performance will rapidly improve.

Think

The first step is to think about and identify traits that are holding you back. What do you need to work on? Once you identify them, pick one or two items and focus your energy on improving those areas. It's important to focus on one or two facets at a time, since this is how we learn best. You must log repetitions to create the paths in the snow. Working on too many will prolong the time it takes to solidify these paths and achieve improvements.

In my previous book, *Feel Younger Now*, I revive an old concept that it takes 21 days to make a habit. This comes from research done by Dr. Maxwell Maltz who wrote the bestseller *Psycho-Cybernetics*. Dr. Maltz, a plastic surgeon, noticed that it took 21 days for amputees to cease feeling the phantom sensations in their amputated limb. In addition, he found that he could apply this 21-day paradigm to shift a patient's self-image, thereby avoiding some plastic surgeries altogether.

While there is no definitive research showing that 21 days is magic and works for every person or every habit, it is certain that habits take multiple days and even weeks or months to create.

Furthermore, replacing bad habits or scripts may take more time than establishing a new script where none existed. That's why it is often easier to learn something correctly from the start, as opposed to correcting mistakes later—after they become scripted and automatic. Limiting your focus to one or two habits at a time will help change or build those habits faster. And the earlier you start, the less you will need to correct old habits.

It's time for you to take the first step in the Think-Play-Send process and determine areas that will help you improve most quickly.

I recently spoke with one of my climbing partners about our weaknesses. He suggested that I sometimes climb too slowly and tend to take the climb straight on—frog style. I agreed. To improve, I should work on climbing more quickly between stances, and develop other techniques like back-stepping.

One way to determine aspects to work on is to query those familiar with you and your climbing. Ask what things they would point out as areas for improvement. I know most of us don't like to hear that we have things to improve on. Our egos feel hammered when this happens. You have to let go of your ego, be open to feedback and then figure out how to improve. People who perform at very high levels in any sport are always very good at taking constructive criticism and learning from it.

So, ask and listen. Don't try and defend why you do what you do. Just listen. Write down what partners suggest. Look for areas pointed out by more than one person—chances are, those are what you need to work on.

Think Exercise #1:

Comments from Friend A:

_____

_____

_____

Comments from Friend B:

_____

_____

Comments from Friend C:

_____

_____

_____

Circle one or two items from the lists above. These are the areas you will work on.

Sometimes your friends can't spot your weaknesses. For example, if you never shared your feelings with them, they may be unaware of your fear of failure. To help self-identify areas for improvement, it may be helpful to write down three or four of your best and three or four of your worst climbing performances. You can do so in the space below.

Best performances:

_____

_____

_____

Worst performances:

_____

_____

_____

_____

Review the list below and self-identify items on the list that played a significant role in each of your best and worst performances noted above. Write them next to the associated performance. For example, you might feel that your precise footwork played a major role in a great onsight. Likewise, you may feel that your fear of falling caused you to blow an onsight.

Fear of falling	Back stepping
Precise footwork	Reading sequences
Climbing faster	Intuitive climbing
Dealing with distractions	Relaxing your grip
Making clips	Dynamic movement
Fear of failure	Traversing on lead
Resting	Remembering beta

In *Performance Rock Climbing*, Goddard and Neumann presented a similar exercise, with more focus on physical and technique issues (e.g., pinches, overhangs). It's a great exercise and even better if you extend it to the mental factors we've discussed.

Using the information you collected, which areas would you benefit most from addressing?

_____

_____

_____

_____

Now you have identified one or two areas that need work—targets that will give you the biggest bang for your buck and help you improve the fastest.

In the next section, you will define exercises to help you improve in these areas—ones that allow learning in a safe and controlled environment. You will safely and effectively begin creating those paths in the snow.

Play

In order to develop good habits or break old habits that hold you back, you need to perform exercises in safety and not in an emotionally-charged atmosphere. You will play, which will help you create new scripts. You will allow yourself to fail and try again. And again. And again. The *objective will not be performance*, but rather the repetition of movements or thoughts that rewire the current scripts running in your mind.

The following are some play exercises (in addition to those introduced in previous chapters) that will help improve on the weaknesses you identified. If you cataloged an item that is not on the list, then contact us at www.masterrockclimber.com, and we'll create a play activity for the new item and might even add it to our list when we revise this book! Just use the contact page and leave a comment.

Find the exercises that correspond to the areas you identified and practice them as described in the corresponding section below.

Fear of falling

If you selected fear of falling and you have not completed the fear of falling profile in Chapter 5, then do so now, as you will have a better idea of how you feel about falling. Most of us do not like to fall, so you're not alone. To improve though, it's important to recognize that you will need to be comfortable falling when appropriate.

If your fear of falling profile shows that you are uncomfortable falling, even when the fall has very low risk of injury, chances are you feel this way because you have not experienced many falls. Your brain sees falling as a great unknown and doesn't have a large enough database of safe falls—your falling script is holding you back. In this case, you need to build the database of falls and rewrite your script.

Return to Chapter 6 and practice the drills described in the *Falling Is Fun* and *The Falling Habit* sections.

It is also possible that you selected fear of falling as a hindrance despite a fear of falling profile that indicates you're comfortable taking safe falls. In this instance, it's likely that intellectually you're comfortable, but you lack a strong database of falls to be relaxed while actually falling. Perhaps when the going gets tough and you face a possible fall, you yell, "take."

If that's the case, the exercises are the same but you may be able to more quickly move through the first levels of the falling exercises. I would caution you, however, to take time and build that database slowly—the path in the snow is best created by footprints and not a snow blower.

Fear of failure

If you identified fear of failure as an impediment, then you probably expect success on every climb you try—seldom falling or failing. Success is great, but you know from Chapters 7 and 8 that too much success can hold you back.

Experimentation with things you can't do and the failure that is bound to occur are key to accelerated learning. Sure, you can learn by pushing your limits gradually—never or seldom failing—but this is a slow way to grow. Failure in a safe and playful environment is the way to advance your abilities more quickly.

So, how do you overcome the fear of failure? Return to the drills in Chapter 8 and select ones that suit you. Another proven drill is to make yourself fail...a lot. Fail trying—in a setting without expectation of success and where failure is seen as a path to growth. Attempt routes that you are quite sure you cannot do without hanging or falling (top-roping if it minimizes anxiety). I often feel a welcomed sense of relief when jumping on a new redpoint "project" because falls are certain. I feel no pressure to onsight or send.

At either your local gym or favorite crag, select a route that is two or three letter grades harder than you can currently climb without falling. If you climb up to 5.9, it will be a full number grade, since letter grades don't exist for climbs below 5.10. If a 5.11a really challenges you, but you seldom fall, choose a 5.11c or 5.11d. To avoid injury, make sure you are warmed-up and not exhausted. If your climbing partner is also participating in this exercise, choose different routes as doing so eliminates any competition that could interfere with the play aspect of the exercise.

Prior to getting on the route, create the mindset that you will try the route without expectation of flashing it. Tell yourself that, when you fail and have to work through sections, you will embrace the learning because it will make you a better climber. When you fall, use the opportunity to figure out what you could have done better and scope out how to do the sequence. If you do not make it to the top of the climb, it's no big deal. Success is not the point. Instead it is to expose yourself to failing in a safe and playful environment—to develop a path in the snow that includes being comfortable with failure.

I suggest doing this exercise as part of your climbing work-out once a week for four weeks, then take a break. Such difficult climbing is hard on your body, and too much failure can have a negative effect (especially if you enjoy the successes in your climbing). You can work this exercise into your routine a few times a year until you find that you have overcome the fear of failure.

Another useful exercise to eliminate performance anxiety is one I call the ASPORT method (described below):

Imagine that you are at the crux of a climb on which you have previously failed. As you try and relax at the stance below the difficult series of moves, you recall the fall you took the last time. You remember how you got partway into the powerful undercling move and how you could not generate enough power to use it. You think about how hard the route was up to this point and how you don't want to have to come back another day and try this again.

You can feel your legs start to tremble as you start into the crux. You grab the undercling and it doesn't feel any better than you remember. As you try and move your feet up, you feel your body sag, just as it had before. Your hand starts to peel open from the undercling as you begin to fall backwards. You yell "take" and find yourself hanging on the end of the rope looking up at the all-too-familiar section of cliff.

Could it be that the thoughts about your previous failed attempts contributed to your failure on this try? It is not only possible, but likely. Fear of failure may not only keep us from doing certain climbs to avoid damaging our egos, it can also create distracting thoughts that draw our attention away from what is really important on the climb at that moment—the TASK AT HAND.

In fact, all thoughts about failure or success are counterproductive. Thoughts of failure can cause you to become nervous. Like me, you may have experienced this with Elvis legs—frightened jitters that are definitely detrimental to your ability to execute controlled movements. Thoughts about success on the climb may cause you to lose focus and become sloppy. You may take easier sections of the climbing for granted and fall due to a careless mistake or fall even after passing the crux. What really matters during the climb is execution of the task at hand—each and every moment from when you leave the ground to when you clip the anchors.

In the past year, I have experimented with mindfulness—improving my focus on the task at hand—and it has made a big difference in my performance. I am sending climbs faster than ever before and with less angst. When heading to and at the cliff, I keep all thoughts of the outcome out of my mind. This takes practice, but once mastered is not hard.

Once I leave the ground, my entire focus is on thinking about the climbing needed to reach the next stance, planning my strategy, and executing my strategy. I implement the SUPER (Shift focus, Understand the risks, Plan your strategy, Execute your plan, and Relax at the next stance) sequence from Chapter 5 over and over until I reach the anchors.

If I fall on the climb and have to work a section, I focus intensely and precisely on how to use the holds involved. I look at each hold and experiment with how best to use it. I focus on how hard I need to crimp, pull, push, or otherwise use the feature while I am working the move, so that I can prepare myself to do the same on my next attempt. This has accelerated how quickly I send routes.

It's ironic that I've improved my ability to have positive outcomes on routes by trying very hard NOT to think about the outcome. Keeping my attention on the execution of each part of a climb, rather than how well I am doing on the climb, has improved my odds dramatically. I not only climb better, but my climbing days have less anxiety and I have more fun (which is the reason I climb after all).

Have you ever climbed with someone who threw temper tantrums when not climbing well? One of my partners was so mad about struggling on a route that he threw his climbing shoes into the woods. I did not climb with him again. Any technique that helps me extract more joy from my days climbing is worthwhile. This technique enhances joy AND has me climbing better.

Here is the ASPORT process I follow. Give it a try.

- AVOID thoughts of the outcome: Once you start your approach to the climbing area, keep all thoughts about success and failure out of your mind. When you find them creeping into your awareness, shift your attention to how the air smells, how the temperature feels, how the routes around you look. Let all thoughts of success or failure pass without dwelling on them. This will take practice.

- SUPER sequence: Practice going through the SUPER sequence. Shift focus, Understand the risks, Plan your strategy, Execute your plan, and Relax at the next stance. Do this on every route, between each and every stance.

- PAUSE if you fail: If you fail, take a deep breath and relax before hauling yourself up the rope to work out the sequence you fell on. This will minimize your level of excitement, which can hamper your problem-solving abilities.

- OPEN your focus: Before you try cruxy sequences, be sure to open your focus widely to allow you to consider as many options as possible.

- REGISTER feelings: When you figure out how to do the move, practice it several times, focusing on how each hold feels and the movement as a whole. Consciously register what it feels like to do the move. For example, it may require crimping down really hard and using a thumb catch. Consciously register that, so that you will recall it later when it matters.

- TELL your body to do the climbing: When you try the route again, focus your attention on the task at hand the entire way up the route. When you execute the crux move, concentrate on the fine points, recalling what it felt like when you worked it. As you head into the hard moves, let your body do the climbing and focus your mind on executing the precise sequence.

Implementing this ASPORT process will improve your ability to send routes more quickly and decrease any performance anxiety.

Relaxing your grip/overgripping

If you identified relaxing your grip as an area of focus, you probably fail on climbs because your forearms get too pumped. Most of us overgrip holds and this can sap our energy, eliminating power for the crux or the end of the pitch. It doesn't feel natural to grip holds as lightly as possible to save energy for later. We must therefore create a habit of doing so.

To develop this habit, consciously work at lightening your grip to the point of nearly falling off. You should do this on a climb that is not hard for you, so warm-ups are ideal for practice—either on lead or on top-rope, depending on your comfort level. As there's a chance you will fall while doing this, recall the lessons in Chapters 7 and 8 and embrace your training as a process where success equals progress.

When you start on your warm-up climbs, consciously grip each hold as lightly as possible with just enough power to make the initial moves. When you reach the first rest or gear, find a stance and once again focus on gripping the handholds as lightly as possible, to the point where you feel as though you might come off. Stop at that point and notice what that feels like. Do this for each move and each stance as you proceed.

As this exercise is not hard on your body, you can continually practice this exercise on your warm-up climbs, building a strong habit to carry over to pressure-filled send situations.

Precise footwork

For most climbers, the area of focus that will yield the biggest benefit is improving footwork. We propel ourselves with forces generated mostly by our legs. Next time you're at the gym or crag, watch how people use their feet. Often you will see people not solidly placing their feet on the best part of the holds, people having only one foot on a hold at a stance, people tapping their feet on holds as they start into a move. These are poor scripts that, when reprogrammed, significantly improve climbing performance.

To develop precise and powerful footwork, you will concentrate on developing the motor control to precisely place your feet on holds in optimal position. You will work on consciously weighting your feet and truly distributing weight on your feet.

The best exercise for developing precise footwork is the well-known "silent feet" drill. In this drill, practice placing your feet precisely and quietly on each foothold. This drill is best done in a gym, since you can readily hear when you do not place your foot softly on a hold—it goes "clunk." A key is to not take your eyes off your foot and intended foothold until your foot is solidly weighted on the hold. This will initially seem very awkward and will result in slow climbing; but over time, it will feel more comfortable and you will be able to move more quickly.

Like learning to grip holds lightly, practicing precise footwork is not hard on your body. As such, you can practice it on all your warm-up climbs or on traverses.

Resting

Climbing endurance is directly related to the quality of rests. Quality resting, which typically focuses on resting the forearm muscles to avoid a pump, requires engaging only the muscles required to hang on, so that circulation is maximized to the recovering muscles. It also requires breath control to ensure oxygen-rich blood is delivered to the working muscles. Shake out techniques are also useful to recover from accumulating pump.

To develop good resting scripts, you will consciously find rest positions, breathe deeply, and practice relaxing all muscles—except those required to hang on. You can do this on routes or when traversing, but choose a route of appropriate difficulty. A climb that is too easy will prevent you from really being able to get into a real rest position. If a climb is too hard, you won't be able to focus on form and relax enough to create that path in the snow.

Keys to effective resting are:
- Keeping your arms straight and sinking as low as possible, transfer weight onto your skeleton and off as many muscles as possible. To practice this, find positions where you have handholds that are big enough to hold onto without much effort, and where you can alternate hands. It can be a single hold suitable for matching or two holds where you can alternate holding on with each hand. The holds should be in a position where you can stand on footholds that allow you to sink down low enough to hang from straight arms. When in this position, sink as low as you possibly can, letting your weight hang on your bones and joints as much as possible. As you breathe in and out, try and sink lower and lower on each successive breath. Do this for 10 seconds while hanging on by one

hand, then switch to the other and repeat five times. Experiment with this, doing at least ten repetitions per drill.

- Breathing deeply while at a rest. While in a rest position, inhale deeply until your lungs are full, then release your breath until your lungs are empty. As you breathe in and out, try to relax your body, paying attention to your heart rate. As you breathe, you may be able to feel it lowering. Feel relaxation and recovery happen.

- Shaking out to drain oxygen-poor blood from the veins. This enhances circulation of oxygen-rich blood instead of oxygen-poor blood that drain the active muscles. The idea behind all shaking techniques is to increase blood-flow to your working muscles. The basic idea is to put your arm above your head for a few seconds, then drop it below your heart for a few seconds, and then repeat. Eric Hörst labeled this the *G-Tox* method.

When you raise your arm above your head, low-pressure, low-oxygen-content venous blood drains out of your arms with the aid of gravity. This has two benefits. It provides a source of blood that can be re-circulated by your heart and re-oxygenated by your lungs to again provide oxygen-rich blood to the muscles in need. It also drains the venous blood from your veins, making room for oxygen-rich blood pumped from your heart.

When you lower your arm below your heart, the blood pressure increases in the small blood vessels of your arm muscles. This increase in pressure helps get oxygen-rich blood to your working muscles. For a one-minute demonstration, hold one arm above your head while holding your other arm down by your side. After a minute, look at the color of your hands—the lower hand will probably be much more red and flush with blood than the upper. Now quickly drop the overhead hand and feel the rush of fresh blood entering your hand.

Although there is debate about how beneficial this next technique is, I use it and feel it helps. Clench and unclench your hands when they are above your head. This further helps move venous blood out of your arm and back to your heart, using the muscles in your forearm as pumps to squeeze blood back toward your heart.

Another more advanced technique is to inhale deeply while your arm is over your head. This decreases the pressure in your thoracic cavity, which causes your heart to fill more completely with blood prior to pumping it to your lungs and to your working muscles.

To practice these techniques, select a climb three or four letter grades below your current maximum onsight level. If you can currently onsight 5.11d but usually fall on 5.12a, pick a 5.10d or 5.11a. If you are practicing on a bouldering traverse, use holds that make the climbing about this level of difficulty. Identify a few stances on the route where you plan on practicing resting. Climb the route and practice the techniques above. Do so for five to ten shakes of each arm at each rest stances you identified. If one of the stances is not restful, climb through it. No sweat.

I suggest doing this on all of your warm-ups for four weeks or 12 climbing sessions, whichever takes longer. This will build a habit and help you refine your resting techniques in a safe environment, so that you will be able to put them into action when you really need them.

Dynamic movement

Most of us are more comfortable when we can reach holds statically. There are times, however, when this is not the case and dynamic movement—using your momentum— is required. The tricky thing about using momentum is that it's a lot like falling upward or sideways to reach a hold. If you miss the targeted hold, you may indeed fall and this can make the movement uncomfortable. Once again, recall the lessons in Chapters 7 and 8 and embrace your training as a process where progress equals success.

Like the other script-altering exercises in this chapter, you will overcome this disguised fear of falling by exposing yourself to the situation in a safe and playful environment. You will work at making dynamic movements, small ones at first, feeling what it is like to fall upwards and sideways. Experiment with snagging holds during dynamic movements, thereby creating scripts, developing finer motor control and eye-hand coordination. The progression will take you to bigger moves that involve more of your body's momentum. Through this play, you will develop a fondness for moving your body in these ways.

If you are very new to dynamic movements, start with small dynamic movements of your hands while bouldering or while on top-rope. Practice grabbing your next hold in a dynamic fashion. The hold that you're going from and the hold you're going to should be large enough that they are not difficult to hold.

From your current stance, determine your next handhold and which hand you want to grab it with. It should be within two feet of the hold where the hand you will be reaching with is currently situated. When you go to grab it, first let your body sag ever-so-slightly down or away from the wall. As you reach for the hold, generate some momentum toward the hold by pulling inward or toward the target hold. Grab the hold as you reach it and hang on. For some, this will be a difficult exercise. Not only may it be uncomfortable for you, but it requires more hand strength than statically latching holds. However, learning this technique will allow you to save energy wasted in locking off statically and allow you to reach holds that would otherwise be out of reach.

If you have some experience with dynamic movement and are looking to get more comfortable with bigger moves, an exercise similar to the one just described can teach you to generate increased momentum with more of your body. To do this, you will need to identify a move that has large holds that are separated by more than two feet—this may be difficult to do on real rock but should be easy in a climbing gym. When you make the move to the target hold, first let your body sag down or away from the wall enough so that you can generate the required momentum to reach the next hold. Reaching the next hold will require generating significant power from your legs. This will take some practice and can be very hard for some. As with the less-advanced exercise, grab the hold as you reach it and hang on. It may be difficult to latch, depending on your strength and how your body momentum is directed.

Another variant on this is to practice easy double-handed dynos from one set of holds to another, with your feet staying firmly on their starting holds. This forces proper body movement and also helps refine your timing and coordination. The movement can be described as generating a "wave" through your body. You start with your hands on a lower hold or set of holds, then push with your legs as both hands simultaneously leave the starting holds and reach for a target hold or holds. Your legs push your hips up and in toward the wall as your shoulders trace an arc outward and back into the hold or holds. The movement is a bit like a snake striking.

I suggest practicing this during one of your climbing workouts each week for four weeks. Do this on your warm-up climbs, doing 20 or more dynamic movements per session. After four weeks, take a break of at least two weeks, as dynamic climbing can be hard on your body. As your comfort with dynamic movement improves, experiment with larger and more dynamic moves.

Climbing faster

If you began climbing two decades ago, when most climbing was done with traditional protection, you probably cultivated a static style and may have developed strong scripts that make it difficult for you to climb quickly.

Learning how to climb quickly when it helps you conserve energy is an important skill. Rapid movement up an entire route, however, is usually more tiring than climbing slowly. It is therefore important to develop the skill of climbing quickly between rest stances, with a rhythm that helps you move with optimal efficiency.

To practice this, identify a route that you have climbed and know—one that is not too difficult (maybe one or two number grades below your onsight ability) and contains several good rest stances. When you climb the route, try and climb as quickly as you can between rests. When you reach a stance, pause and rest for at least ten seconds before quickly climbing to the next stance.

Practice this until you feel smooth when climbing quickly. This exercise is best left for your second or third warm-up, as it's best to initially warm up gently. It may take several weeks for you to feel smooth, but if you practice this exercise each time you climb, you will get there.

Learning to climb faster has additional benefits. Rather than grabbing a hold and stopping over and over, you can generate momentum from move to move. The momentum makes each move easier, conserving even more energy.

Back-stepping

Many climbers have learned how to climb with the traditional "X" or "frog" style— facing into the wall with knees turned out to the sides. This is a very effective body position in many climbing situations, especially when the angle is vertical or less. However, on overhanging terrain there are many cases where the use of a back-step will make a move much easier. A back-step would be where you pull hardest with your left hand while standing on the outside edge of your right foot, rotating your lower body so that your right hip is against the wall, and your other leg is positioned big toe closest to the wall.

Back-stepping is very useful when in a rest position because it often allows you to more easily keep your arm straight, due to the resulting twist in your body. It is also useful in making progress on steep terrain. The twist in your body that results when you back-step turns the hip and shoulder side of your reaching arm into the wall, enabling you to reach higher. The oppositional forces generated by your legs also allows you to push more effectively with your legs, while holding your body against the wall. Finally, back-stepping on overhanging terrain can help you overcome the barn-door swing you would feel in the traditional "frog" position.

Practicing back-stepping is quite simple. On your warm-up climbs, look for every opportunity to experiment with the back-step body position. See how many times you can back-step on a route. Play with it; experiment with back-steps in unlikely positions.

I suggest practicing this during at least one of your warm-up climbs, each time you climb until your back-stepping feels natural. It may take several weeks to feel comfortable back-stepping but practicing adds to your cache of climbing tricks.

Traversing on lead

If you've been lead climbing for a while, you've likely en-countered a situation where you must lead across a traverse. This can be unsettling, triggering scripts that have us overgripping or yelling "take." Even if you are comfortable falling in a typical downward-fall situation, traversing can feel spooky. The plain and simple reason is that you don't encounter the situation all that often, so your database on the topic is rather lean.

To increase the depth of your database and become comfort-able with it, you need to put yourself in this position many times. Practice is even more powerful if you experience falls in this sit-uation and come to understand what to expect. You can modify the "Fear of Falling" drill from Chapter 6 to include falls where your body is not in line with the bolt you are falling onto. As with the previous drill, you should start small and build up experience to successfully create a useful script to help you with this.

Dealing with distractions

Ever snap at your belayer, yell at a barking dog, or feel an-noyed by a screaming kid? Unless you are some sort of saint, I'll bet that you have. When we are anxious, our senses are height-ened and it is very easy for us to tune into distracting sounds and sights. These distractions pull our attention away from where it really belongs, on the task at hand—climbing.

Sometimes the distractions can be healthy. Hearing your partner scream because there is a snake next to him can actu-ally be a good thing. It may be a good idea for you to know this while he changes positions and deals with the threat. Many times though, as discussed in previous chapters, these distractions are not useful and merely take your attention away from climbing. That barking dog is not really going to interfere with you doing the crux move, is it? Is that tug on the rope from your inattentive belayer going to make you fall? Most times not.

In order to learn to deal with distractions, consciously rehearse focusing your attention on the tasks at hand—creating a new mindfulness script. When distractions occur, welcome them as an opportunity to practice the art of staying focused. You will thank that dog for barking because it allows you to practice your ability to stay focused. You will thank your partner for the slight short-rope.

The drill for building focus while climbing is quite simple. While climbing, focus all of your attention on each and every move; consciously feel the texture of each handhold; feel the pressure on your feet; sense the breath flowing in and out of your lungs; absorb yourself in every sensation of climbing. The best way to avoid distraction is to direct your full attention onto something. This drill may initially be difficult for some, as we are so used to letting distractions rule our attention that it is hard to find our focus. If you practice this technique on all your climbs, it will eventually be the way that you always climb.

Reading sequences

Solving the puzzles of movement is one aspect of climbing that many of us enjoy. It's really fun to figure out a perplexing move and then pull it off. A key to this is having the ability to read sequences before you are in the middle of them. Some people are naturally better at this than others, but if you are one of those for whom it does not come naturally, fear not. You can learn to do this.

One of the best ways to build the capability to read sequences is to force yourself to read them from the safest place—the ground. Step back and visually inspect the route prior to climbing. Try to identify handholds and footholds. Which hand will you have on which hold? Are there places where you think you will need to match hands or feet? Where are the rests? Where is the crux? What do you envision doing in that blank section or at that roof?

Climb the route in your mind and actually visualize doing the moves as you think they will be done. It may be helpful to pantomime the hand positions you will use. It will be clearer what to do low on the climb and more questionable up high where you can't see details. Nonetheless, try to envision what you think awaits you. Doing this will develop your ability to visualize moves and prepare you for what to do on the climb.

Twelve feet up the climb, you may find that you were wrong. That's okay. Just like in battle, you may find that your plan isn't right, but the exercise of planning is valuable anyway. Not having a plan heading into battle would be considered suicide. Okay, it's not as dramatic when climbing a route, but it is valuable nonetheless.

Remembering beta →Visualization

There are a number of tricks that can improve your ability to remember beta. They all rely on visualization, which is perhaps the archetype for mental training. The first step is to figure out the beta—the topic of the prior section on reading sequences. The second step is to encode that information. Encoding refers to the process of transferring information from working memory/short-term memory to long-term memory. Studies in cognitive psychology demonstrate that we are more likely to remember things that are encoded in multiple forms, such as words and images. This is an extremely important point that leads to our first trick: When it comes to beta, you should visualize holds, visualize moves, feel in your body what it is like to make the move, and describe all of these in words. That's why the "R" in ASPORT is so important; it means Register all of this information consciously, allowing you to encode it in multiple forms.

The second trick is to make the verbal description more explicit. Options include discussing it with other climbers, practicing similar moves, or writing it down. For really challenging redpoints, the latter can be very effective. Writing out beta is a form of memory—think of it as external storage. In case you forget moves, re-read your description. And writing has another huge advantage—it exposes gaps in your memory: "Left hand to sloper, right hand to pinch . . . a miracle occurs . . . and I stick the dyno." It's those little "miracle occurs" sections that are most likely to send you airborne on the redpoint attempt. If you can't write down the foot sequence, then you don't know it.

The third trick is the visualization process itself. You need to repeat it over and over. I will routinely visualize every single move I can remember from leaving the ground to clipping the anchor, three times per day between climbing trips. I don't just visualize the holds; I picture all the clips and rests, even chalking. In Chapter 2, we discussed the benefits of scripts and automaticity, but another major psychological finding is that visualization activates the same areas of the brain as actually doing the action. For example, closing your eyes and visualizing holds activates the occipital cortex, the brain's vision area. Visualizing a movement activates the same somatosensory cortical areas as doing the movement. In other words, you are putting Hebb's Law to work for you.

As it turns out, we tend to retrieve memories the same way we encode and practice them, leading to our fourth trick. When you do your daily visualizations, pull out all the stops: Close your eyes to picture the holds, flex the same muscles, pantomime the movements, make the clips, practice relaxing, and talk yourself through the moves out loud. Oh, and don't forget to clip the chains! It may look and sound silly, but it absolutely works. If embarrassment is holding you back, then re-read Chapter 7, or practice in a closet.

As climbers, we are lucky. Visualization is more effective in climbing than in many other sports. Why? Because our medium is static. We aren't up against an unpredictable opponent. Unless the holds break, climbs stay the same. We can visualize while we are at home and accurately anticipate what we will encounter, as opposed to the tennis player or basketball player who never knows what his opponent's next move will be.

The first time I really put visualization to the test was on my first 5.12c, *The Gem*, at Shelf Road. I worked the beta one weekend and reviewed it from the ground. I practiced via visualization every day, at home and at work. When I returned the following weekend, I hiked the route. In fact, it felt too easy! I was tired when I worked out the beta, so that's how I remembered it: "Reach really far for the pocket." But when I actually did the moves fresh, I found myself reaching past the holds because the moves were easier than I'd visualized.

A final benefit to visualization is one that applies to many of the mental tips we have provided—it only requires your brain and time. You won't wear out your fingertips, or pull a tendon, or make your muscles sore. In fact, you can continue to improve your performance even when your muscles are sore, after workouts or on rest days.

Making clips

Does the rope get incredibly heavy when you go to make a clip? Do you lose motor control of your fingers when clipping? This happens to many of us. It seems like an eternity as we pull up that loop of rope, exposing us to an even longer fall should we blow it. It can be a frightening moment. It is the fumbling that poses the greatest risk and often our rush to make a clip is what causes this fumbling. Going slowly can actually be faster at times like these.

As with our other exercises, it is best to learn how to clip efficiently and effectively in a safe environment—on easy climbs. Better yet, hang a quickdraw next to your favorite living room chair, grab a short section of rope, and clip in total safety. In this environment you can practice slowly and deliberately making clips. Practice clipping with either hand and in various positions. You can experience clipping above your head and at your waist. You can experiment with different ways of manipulating the rope into the carabiner. Do this on all of the warm-up climbs that you lead. It will help you develop the scripts of having the fine motor skills and techniques that enable you to quickly and efficiently clip, even in stressful situations.

On harder climbs, the decisions about where to place protection or from which holds to clip a bolt become more important. On trad routes, where you are placing your protection, you are on your own. Your decision to place protection is based on a compromise between the best placements and the best stances. You will save energy if you can safely climb to a good stance. Stopping too often or at bad stances creates a snowball effect. You waste energy, get more pumped, become less confident to run it out, and stop more often, wasting more energy…. Climbing the unrelenting splitter cracks of Indian Creek epitomizes this negative-feedback loop.

On sport climbs, you have the luxury of pre-placed bolts, but you still have to decide which holds to use while clipping. In general, experienced route developers compromise between where they feel a bolt is most needed and where it can be most easily clipped. Some climbs don't offer great clipping options, especially in sustained sections. In any case, developers usually place bolts with the intent that they be clipped when you are just below the bolt or when it is at head-level. Keep this in mind as you approach the next bolt. Stretching to clip a bolt from the lowest possible hold can backfire. You are likely to waste energy straining to make the reach, you will have to pull up extra rope, and you may be missing the best clipping holds.

If you are comfortable that you won't fall or that a fall would be safe, you can save energy by waiting until your hands are above the bolt, possibly even waiting until it is at your hip. This way you pull up less rope or none at all.

Does this put you at risk for a longer fall? Probably not. If you do the math, the fall distance is the same whether you clip at your hip or pull up several feet of slack to clip over your head.

An example will illustrate the math. Imagine your next bolt is three feet above the one you just clipped. You have two options:

1. Climb until you can reach it from below. Let's say this puts the bolt you already have clipped exactly at your waist. If you fall now, you have no extra slack and your fall is zero feet—ignoring rope stretch and slack from your drowsy belayer. You would need to pull up six feet of slack, a tiring process, in order to clip (three feet from waist to bolt + three feet from bolt back to your harness). If you fall just as you're clipping, you will go six feet.
2. Climb until the next bolt is at your waist. Since the bolts are three feet apart, your waist is now three feet above the bolt you already have clipped. However, you don't need to pull slack, thus conserving strength. If you can't clip or you fall while clipping, you will go six feet (from three feet above the first bolt to three feet below it).

In either case, you fall the same distance. However, the second option can conserve energy. I'm especially likely to do this high on an overhanging route where I know I could fall 50 feet without injury.

Option #2 has another benefit when you are close to the ground or above a ledge. Your instincts tell you option #1 is safer—the sooner you clip the better! Not true. All things being equal (meaning the holds), you are safer with option #2 because you are less likely to hit the ground or ledge. That may sound like it contradicts my claim that you will fall the same distance. It doesn't. If you fall the same distance, six feet in this example, but you start the fall from three feet higher, then you will finish the fall three feet higher. In option #1, you end up six feet below the first bolt. (Imagine standing right at the bolt with six feet of slack in your hand and jumping off.) In option #2, you end up three feet below the first bolt. That could make all the difference between a safe fall versus broken legs—or worse.

Intuitive climbing

To climb intuitively is to have instinct—or well-wired scripts. Intuitive climbing comes in very handy when you climb up and into an area where it is not clear what you need to do. When you climb intuitively, you know what to do without having to think much. You may have experienced intuition when you came to a spot on a climb, and although it wasn't obvious what to do, you managed to grab for a handhold that happened to be good. You didn't slap your hands around on all the possible features. You just reached out and boom, there was the hold.

Intuition is the act or faculty of knowing immediately, directly, and holistically without the use of reasoning and without being aware of how we know. Intuition is related to confidence in that when there is no absolute right or wrong, you have the confidence to proceed without thinking through and confirming that what you are doing is correct. Instead of thinking about it, you act in a way that feels right and you follow through with confidence. You need to quickly invoke the technique scripts required by each move. Recalling the previous discussions about the power of automaticity, intuitive climbing depends heavily on having a large library of automatic responses.

Developing your climbing intuition involves climbing confidently without much thought to whether the way you are climbing a route is "right" or not. You grab holds, move your feet up and go directly into the next move. Once you start into whatever move you attempt, you follow through with it and don't stop midway if it feels wrong. The best way to develop your intuitive climbing ability is to do so while bouldering or on a top-rope, where falling has little or no consequences. Climbing intuitively fosters faster climbing and vice versa.

Unlike in some of the previous exercises, do not preview the route or try to figure out and plan the sequences. Instead, begin climbing and keep moving, without pausing to think about what to do. Use your sense of sight to spot the next hold, but try not to assess the body positions. Just climb. This can be a tiring exercise and you may fall, but that is okay. Success is not the point. You are playing and learning. I suggest practicing this on two or three routes per climbing session until it feels smooth and easy. At this point, you should be able to climb routes within a number grade of your onsight level in this manner, without falling.

Send

In the "Think" section of this chapter, you identified one or two areas that would yield the biggest improvements when mastered. Then, in the "Play" section, you focused your training on those areas—practicing exercises in a safe and playful environment to form new paths in the snow, new habits in the areas that you identified. In this final "Send" section, you will solidify the new habits that you created. You will apply them to the real-world situation of trying to send a route under the pressures of difficult moves, pumped arms, and potential falls. This will have the effect of making them useful in similar situations, when you really need them. It doesn't much matter whether you are trying to onsight or redpoint. What matters is that you really want to climb the route well, to send it, and that it is challenging for you. The emotions that emerge because of your enthusiasm and the fact that you will be challenged create the right environment for you to put into practice your new scripts and move them even deeper into your subconscious as automata.

So, find a route that you are excited about and that will be challenging for you, and climb it, drawing upon the new habits that you have formed on top of your previously existing skills. The following is an example of how you might experience your newly created habits.

The route is named *Lats Have No Feelings*, and you have wanted to onsight it for a few years, but have avoided it because you have never felt up to it. Today, you will attempt to onsight *Lats*. Succeed or not, you really want to climb the route. You have been working on trying to not get caught up in the result, and instead focus on the journey. You're able to put that training into practice today and go for it, putting aside your *fear of failure.*

Before you rope up, you walk about five yards away from the base of the climb and *scope out where the route goes.* The bottom 20 or 30 feet look reasonable, with pretty obvious flakes and cracks that weave between the bolts. It looks like you will get a rest at around 30 feet on a ledge, which is great. The next 30-foot section is hard to read from the ground, but appears to involve laybacking a mini-arête, which has some serious chalky spots. They are probably either rest holds or cruxes, but by the looks of them, you guess rest holds. You have to step back to get a decent look above that. There looks to be a series of underclings up to a fairly featureless finishing face. You guess that there must be holds up there, but they are just too high to see. You'll try and *read the sequences* when you get closer.

You rope up, do a safety check with your belayer, and start climbing. As you had suspected, the climbing is not very difficult. You climb *quickly and smoothly* up to the ledge at 30 feet, clipping the bolts along the way. On the ledge, you are able to *cop a great rest* and totally de-pump. The route appears to traverse to the left from the nice ledge rest. You scope out the potential fall situation and convince yourself that there is nothing to hit and that any swing this high up will be totally safe.

You open your focus and spot some *key footholds*, which gives you confidence that you know the sequence to get to the next stance and clip. You do the moves, *using the key small footholds with precision.* You find the stance, hang the quickdraw and *clip the rope* through it smoothly, hearing the satisfying "click" as the gate snaps shut. Alright, the climbing above looks like it could be hard. As you're trying to work out the moves above, two dogs get into a fight about 50 feet from your belayer. In the past, you would have been shaken by the commotion. Today, you let it pass, without another thought. *You bring your focus back to the climbing ahead.*

You have an idea of how to proceed, but you're not sure it's right. You take two quick breaths and begin climbing, acting. You move quickly and smoothly, *clipping the next three bolts with ease*. When you reach a series of underclings, the pump in your forearms builds. You know that you can't spend too much time there figuring out what to do. You *open your focus* and look at the options. You see what looks like a decent hold, but it is out of reach. You look down and behind you and see an opportunity to back-step, which will help you get the height to reach the suspected good hold. Two breaths and you are moving.

You find the back-step and it is just the ticket to get you to what ends up being a pretty good hold. Not great, but good enough to move your feet and quickly clip the next bolt. By now, you are beginning to fade. You don't have time to think, so you get your feet up and *intuitively bump your left hand up dynamically*, around a blind bulge. Your mind rejoices when your left hand finds a huge and positive pocket. Ka-ching! You move your feet up again and find a nice series of jugs that leads to the chain anchors. You did it!

This is an example that illustrates how you can put a variety of newly formed habits to work while sending routes. Each time you tap into one of these habits in the emotionally-packed environment of a challenging route, it moves the habit deeper and deeper into your subconscious, making it an even more automatic response. As mentioned at the beginning of this chapter, you can run through the Think-Play-Send process as many times as you like, each time selecting the things in your climbing that you feel need work. Each time through, your habits will get stronger and stronger and your climbing better and better.

We hope that you put the training suggestions we presented into action. If you do, then chances are you will see rapid improvements in your climbing performance. It's also likely that you will extract more joy from climbing. If you want to find more training advice, visit **www.masterrockclimber.com** where there is a load of free training material in the "*Free stuff*" tab. Enjoy the journey. Climb on!

12 References

References

Chapter 1:

Ilgner, A. (2006). *The rock warriors way: Mental training for rock climbers.* La Vergne, TN: Desiderata Institute.

McGrath, D., Medic, N., & Wright, V. (2010). *50 athletes over 50 teach us to live a strong, healthy life.* Fort Collins, CO: Wise Media Group.

Chapter 2:

Ashcraft, M. A., & Radvansky, G. A. (2009). *Cognition* (5th ed.). Upper Saddle River, NJ: Pearson.

Ellis, A., & Dryden, W. (2007). *The practice of Rational Emotive Therapy* (2nd ed.). New York: Springer.

Goddard, D., & Neumann, U. (1993). *Performance rock climbing.* Mechanicsburg, PA: Stackpole Books.

Schank, R. C., & Abelson, R. P. (1977). *Scripts, plans, goals and understanding: An inquiry into human knowledge structures.* Oxford England: Lawrence Erlbaum.

Tomkins, S. S. (1991). *Affect/imagery/consciousness. Vol. 3: The negative affects: Anger and fear.* New York: Springer.

Chapter 3:

Atkinson, J., & Feather, N. (1966). A theory of achievement motivation. New York: Wiley and Sons.

Csíkszentmihályi, M. (1990). *Flow: The psychology of optimal experience.* New York: HarperCollins.

Decker, L. (2009). *Motivation: Biological, psychological, and environmental* (3rd ed.). Upper Saddle River, NJ: Pearson.

Erikson, E. H. (1994). *Identity and the life cycle.* New York: Norton. (Original work published 1959)

Gilbert, D. (2007). *Stumbling on happiness.* New York: Vintage.

Harter, S. (1978). Effectance motivation reconsidered: Toward a developmental model. *Human Development, 1,* 34-64.

Konnor, M. (2010). *The evolution of childhood: Relationships, emotion, mind.* Boston: Belknap Press of Harvard University Press.

McClelland, D. C. (1961) *The achieving society.* New York: Free Press.

McGrath, D., Medic, N., & Wright, V. (2010), *50 athletes over 50 teach us to live a strong, healthy life.* Fort Collins, CO: Wise Media Group.

Tomkins, S. S. (1962). *Affect/imagery/consciousness. Vol. 1: The positive affects.* New York: Springer.

Tomkins, S. S. (1963). *Affect/imagery/consciousness. Vol. 2: The negative affects.* New York: Springer.

Wilson, E. O. (1984). *Biophilia.* Boston: Harvard University Press.

Zuckerman, M. (1979). *Sensation seeking: beyond the optimal level of arousal.* Hillsdale, NJ: Lawrence Erlbaum.

Zuckerman, M. (2007). *Sensation seeking and risky behavior.* Washington, D.C.: American Psychological Association.

Chapter 4:

Decker, L. (2009). *Motivation: Biological, psychological, and environmental* (3rd ed.). Upper Saddle River, NJ: Pearson.

Kalat, J. W., & Shiota, M. N. (2011). *Emotion.* Belmont, CA: Wadsworth.

Vohs, K. D., & Baumeister, R. F. (2011). *Handbook of self-regulation: Research, theory, and applications (2nd ed.).* New York, NY: Guilford.

Chapter 5:

Kalat, J. W., & Shiota, M. N. (2011). *Emotion.* Belmont, CA: Wadsworth.

Schank, R. C., & Abelson, R. P. (1977). *Scripts, plans, goals and understanding: An inquiry into human knowledge structures.* Oxford England: Lawrence Erlbaum.

Chapter 6:

Benson, H., & Klipper, M. Z. (2001). *The relaxation response.* New York: HarperCollins.

Kalat, J. W., & Shiota, M. N. (2011). *Emotion.* Belmont, CA: Wadsworth.

Chapter 7:

Conroy, D. E. (2001). Progress in the development of a multidimensional measure of fear of failure: The Performance Failure Appraisal Inventory (PFAI). *Anxiety, Stress & Coping: An International Journal, 14(4),* 431-452.

Conroy, D. E. (2004). The unique psychological meanings of multidimensional fears of failing. *Journal of Sport & Exercise Psychology, 26(3),* 484-491.

Cooley, C. H. (1902). *Human nature and the social order.* New York: Charles Scribner's Sons.

Eisenberger, N. I., Lieberman, M. D., & Williams, K. D. (2003). Does rejection hurt: An fMRI study of social exclusion. *Science, 302,* 290-292.

Elison, J., & Partridge, J. A. (2012). Relationships between shame-coping, fear of failure, and perfectionism in college athletes. *Journal of Sport Behavior, 35(1),* 19-39.

Leary, M. R., Tambor, E. S., Terdal, S. K., & Downs, D. L. (1995). Self-esteem as an interpersonal monitor: The sociometer hypothesis. *Journal of Personality and Social Psychology, 68(3),* 518-530.

MacLeod, D. (2010). *9 out of 10 climbers make the same mistakes.*

Inverness-shire, Scotland: Rare Breed Productions.

Nathanson, D. L. (1992). *Shame and pride: Affect, sex, and the birth of the self.* New York: Norton.

Sagar, S. S., & Stoeber, J. (2009). Perfectionism, fear of failure, and affective responses to success and failure: The central role of fear of experiencing shame and embarrassment. *Journal of Sport and Exercise Psychology, 31,* 602-627.

Scheff, T. J. (1988). Shame and conformity: The deference-emotion systems. *American Sociological Review, 53,* 395-406.

Chapter 8:

Adams, C. E., & Leary, M. R. (2007). Promoting self-compassionate attitudes toward eating among restrictive and guilty eaters. *Journal of Social & Clinical Psychology, 26(10),* 1120-1144.

Bandura, A. (1997). *Self-efficacy: The exercise of control.* New York: W.H. Freeman/Times Books/Henry Holt & Co.

Elison, J., Lennon, R., & Pulos, S. (2006). Investigating the compass of shame: The development of the Compass of Shame Scale, Social Behavior and Personality, 34, 221-238.

Elison, J., & Partridge, J. A. (2012). Relationships between shame-coping, fear of failure, and perfectionism in college athletes. *Journal of Sport Behavior, 35(1),* 19-39.

Goddard, D., & Neumann, U. (1993). *Performance rock climbing.* Mechanicsburg, PA: Stackpole Books.

Hewitt, P. L., & Flett, G. L. (1991). Perfectionism in the self and social context: Conceptualization, assessment, and association with psychopathology. *Journal of Personality and Social Psychology, 60,* 456-470.

Hill, R. W., Huelsman, T. J., Furr, R. M., Kibler, J., Vicente, B. B., & Kennedy, C. (2004). A new measure of perfectionism: The Perfectionism Inventory. *Journal of Personality Assessment, 82,* 80-91.

Neff, K. D. (2003). The development and validation of a scale to measure self-compassion. *Self and Identity, 2(3)*, 223-250.

Neff, K. D. (2011). *Self-compassion: Stop beating yourself up and leave insecurity behind.* New York: William Morrow.

Price, K., & Elison, J. (2009, April). *Shame and self-compassion.* Paper presented at the Rocky Mountain Psychological Association convention, Albuquerque, NM.

Chapter 9:

Bandura, A. (1997). *Self-efficacy: The exercise of control.* New York: W.H. Freeman/Times Books/Henry Holt & Co.

Goddard, D., & Neumann, U. (1993). *Performance rock climbing.* Mechanicsburg, PA: Stackpole Books.

MacLeod, D. (2010). *9 out of 10 climbers make the same mistakes.* Inverness-shire, Scotland: Rare Breed Productions.

Vygotsky, L. S. (1978). *Mind in society: The development of higher psychological processes.* Boston: Harvard University Press.

Chapter 10:

Csíkszentmihályi, M. (1990). *Flow: The psychology of optimal experience.* New York: HarperCollins.

McGrath, D., Medic, N., & Wright, V. (2010). *50 athletes over 50 teach us to live a strong, healthy life.* Fort Collins, CO: Wise Media Group.

Hooper, H. (1999). *Affective and motivational components of the flow state: Rock climbing revisited.* (Master's thesis). University of North Dakota: Grand Forks, ND.

Chapter 11:

Ashcraft, M. A., & Radvansky, G. A. (2009). *Cognition* (5th ed.). Upper Saddle River, NJ: Pearson.

Goddard, D., & Neumann, U. (1993). *Performance rock climbing.* Mechanicsburg, PA: Stackpole Books.

Horst, E. J. (2008). *Training for rock climbing: The definitive guide to improving your performance* (2nd ed.). Helena, MT: FalconGuides.

Maltz, M. (1989). *Psycho-cybernetics, a new way to get more living out of life.* New York: Pocket Books.

Maltz, M. (2002). *New psycho-cybernetics.* Upper Saddle River, NJ: Prentice Hall.

McGrath, D. (2012). *Feel younger – now! 21 days, 7 habits.* Denver, CO: 50 Interviews, Inc.

Jeff Elison is a father, author, speaker, rock climber, and professor of psychology. Jeff loves rock climbing of all sorts (bouldering, sport, traditional) and continues to use the tips presented here to improve his mental game—a never ending task. He completed his doctorate in 2003 at the University of Northern Colorado and a NIMH postdoctoral fellowship at the University of Denver in 2005. Since then, he has been teaching and doing research. His research focuses on motivation and emotion, in particular, self-conscious emotions, such as embarrassment, shame, guilt, and humiliation. Jeff lives in the San Luis Valley of Colorado, where he teaches psychology at Adams State University.

Jeff can be reached by email at:
jeff_elison@msn.com

Don McGrath is an author, speaker, trainer, avid rock climb-er, and business leader who enjoys helping people achieve high-performance, whether it be in their sport, business or other parts of their life. Don's first book, *50 Athletes Over 50*, explores the mindsets and strategies employed by active people over age 50 to stay active and extremely healthy. His website, *masterrockclimb-er.com* is devoted to helping rock climbers train more effectively, both physically and mentally. Don lives with his wife Sylvia in Colorado.

Don can be reached by email at:
don@50interviews.com

Photo Captions by Page Number

Opening page: a. Miwa Oba near Lincoln Lake, photo: Susanica Tam; b. Same as page 17; c. Chris Sharma, always in the spotlight, rests and waits for his turn to compete, photo: Susanica Tam; d. Jess relaxing in Boulder Canyon, photo: Jim Thornburg.

p 5: Hans Florine totally focused while speed climbing *The Nose* on El Capitan, CA. Photo: Jim Thornburg

p 17: Stephen Meinhold hits the sloper on *Mango Tango* 5.14a at the New River Gorge, WV. Photo: Jim Thornburg

p 45: Paul Robinson (foreground) and Daniel Woods wait for their turn to compete at the first Bouldering World Cup held in the United States, at the Teva Mountain Games, June 5-9, 2008 in Vail, CO. Robinson's performance at the competition earned him a 3rd place finish that day. Photo: Susanica Tam

p 69: Ben Moon battling the fright factor on *Scirocco* (5.12a) in the Needles, CA. Photo: Jim Thornburg

p 85: Jason Campbell takes a huge whipper on *Cowboy King* 5.13b, Wild Iris, WY. Photo: Jim Thornburg

p 105: Cody Simms hoping the 20-year-old pin will hold on *Twilight Zone* (5.13a), Shawangunks, NY. Photo: Jim Thornburg

p 119: Sonnie Trotter slips off a project near Redstone, Colorado. Photo: Jon Jonkers

p121: Angie Payne reacts to falling off a boulder problem during the World Cup qualifiers at the Teva Mountain Games in Vail, Colo. in 2008. Payne is a seasoned climber that has been competing since her youth and has found a way to have fun and excel at the same time. Photo: Susanica Tam

p147: Toshi Takeuchi of Japan reigns in his focus and chalks up his hands while his turn to climb during the final round of the 2008 American Bouldering Series championships. Photo: Susanica Tam

p 187: Kiyoshi Yoshida laughs with Dai Koyamada and Miwa Oba after falling during an attempt to climb a boulder on Mt. Sanitas near Boulder, Colorado. Photo: Susanica Tam

p 215: The legendary Lynn Hill focuses her attention during an onsight attempt of *Anarchitect* (5.12d), Clear Creek Canyon, CO. Photo: Fred Knapp

p 229: Joel Love putting in big effort on *Le prophete est sur le parking* (5.12d) in Buoux, France. Photo: Jim Thornburg

p 251: Sarah McNichols demonstes a back-step at the Boulder Rock Club. Photo: Fred Knapp

p 265: Daniel Woods takes a fall during the qualifying rounds of the 2008 World Cup. Photo: Susanica Tam

p 272 & 273: Photo of Jeff Elison by Brad Johnson. Photo of Don McGrath by Kirk Donaldson

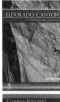

Sharp End Publishing

Authentic Guides From Core Climbers

sharpendbooks.com
(303) 444-2698